WORKSKILLS
Book 2

Susan C. Quatrini

Miami-Dade Community College, Homestead, Florida

Consulting Authors

Mary Lou Beilfuss Byrne
Kathy S. Van Ormer

Prentice-Hall, Inc.

Library of Congress Cataloging-in-Publication Data

Quatrini, Susan C., (date)
  Workskills, Book 2/Susan C. Quatrini ; consulting authors,
Mary Lou Beilfuss Byrne, Kathy S. Van Ormer.
      p.   cm.
    ISBN 0-13-953084-3 (pb) :
    1. English language--Textbooks for foreign speakers.
I. Byrne, Mary Lou Beilfuss, (date). II. Van Ormer, Kathy S., (date)
III. Title.   IV. Title: Workskills book 2.   V. Title : Workskills
book two.
PE1128.Q38 1994
428.2'4--dc20   93-14197
                                              CIP

Acquisitions Editor: Nancy Leonhardt
Managing Editor: Sylvia Moore
Editorial Production/Supervision: Shirley Hinkamp
Pre-Press Production: Infinite Graphics
Cover Illustration: Comstock
Cover Design: Laura Ierardi
Copy Editor: Anne Graydon
Prepress Buyer: Ray Keating
Manufacturing Buyer: Lori Bulwin

Printed in the United States of America

10   9

ISBN 0-13-953084-3

Contents

About the Book

Brief Description of *Workskills*

Workskills is a series of three books and three audiotapes for workplace literacy. The books and tapes are written for students at high beginning (Students are literate.), low intermediate, and high intermediate levels. The books and tapes are coordinated so that they can be used with multi-level groups of students and one teacher. Each book deals with different aspects of the same unit topic.

The approach of the texts is functional, contextual, and problem-solving. The exercises are interactive, cooperative, and practical.

Reading, vocabulary development, speaking, listening, and writing are included. The readings are controlled in length and structure. Basic math skills and graphical literacy are included. Positive work attitudes are developed.

Features of *Workskills*

Each unit contains these features:
Before You Read
Reading About Work (a titled story or dialogue based on the unit theme)
Understanding New Words
Understanding the Reading
Discussing
Reading at Work (including Understanding New Words, a nonfictional reading related to types of reading required at work, and Understanding the Reading)
Writing
Listening
Using Math or Using Graphical Literacy

Teaching with *Workskills*

Before You Read

The unit opening page contains one or more photographs, one or more illustrations, or one or more cartoon frames related to the unit theme. Students examine the photos/illustrations/cartoons and describe what they see. The instructor may wish to list vocabulary suggested by the students. The students continue to work with partners to read, think about and answer the questions on the page. This process helps build on existing vocabulary, relates real work experiences to the lesson, and prepares the students for the reading that follows.

Reading About Work

The **Reading About Work** section includes a fictional story or dialogue that follows the **Before You Read** page and illustrates the unit theme. The stories or dialogues proceed from simple sentences, verb tenses, and grammatical structures to more complex sentences, verb tenses, and grammatical structures. The length of the stories or dialogues gradually increases to help students prepare for the succeeding *Workskills* book(s). The authors chose story settings that represent a variety of workplace situations and/or settings that most students would be familiar with.

Understanding New Words

This feature helps expand and use new vocabulary that was introduced in context in the story or dialogue. Various formats were used throughout *Workskills* to help students find, understand, and practice the new or unfamiliar vocabulary. This section can be used successfully either before or after the story or dialogue, depending on the instructor's preference and the needs of the students.

Understanding the Reading

This feature helps both students and teacher check literal and inferential comprehension of the story or dialogue. Once again, various formats were used in *Workskills* to create and maintain interest. These exercises may be done independently as an assessment, or with a partner or a small group, thus providing more speaking practice.

Discussing

The Discussing portion of the unit provides opportunities for the students to work together on specific activities relating to the story or dialogue and to the unit topic. Students may be asked to complete a conversation, to role play situations they may encounter at the workplace, to solve problems, to evaluate and judge reasons for being late for work, to judge appropriate and inappropriate statements in conversations, etc.

Listening

Each unit of *Workskills* includes a listening activity. The conversations that correspond to the listening activities in the books are found on the accompanying audiotapes for *Workskills* 1,2,3. The types of conversations included are ones that students might hear at work or participate in at work. Most of the conversations involve two co-workers, a supervisor and a worker, or two supervisors. The conversations involve people discussing work-related topics or making "small talk" at work.

The students' tasks in most cases is to listen for specific information. They will need to use this information for various further activities—to fill in a chart or grid, circle or write an answer, take notes, or make judgments. Many times at work, employees are given information that they need to act on. Thus, in some of the listening activities, the students will use the information for further problem-solving activities.

The speech in the conversations is natural and idiomatic. The students will learn that they don't need to understand every word when they are listening for specific information. The exercises will help train the students to pick out only the information pertinent to the task and will also assist them in understanding spoken English in on-the-job situations.

Reading at Work

The Reading at Work section in each unit focuses on the types of readings that an employee might actually encounter on the job: signs, memos, notices on bulletin boards, excerpts from policy and safety manuals, and excerpts from company newsletters. Many of the readings are authentic—at times, they have been modified for the level of *Workskills* in which they are included.

A variety of comprehension activities follows the readings. These include exercises involving literal and inferential comprehension, making judgments and scanning for specific information. Discussion questions relating the readings to the students' jobs are also included. Whenever possible, the instructor should bring in authentic reading materials from the students' worksite. These added realia will personalize the topic and help the employee to understand his company and his job better.

Writing

These materials are designed to teach English through an integrated skills approach. The writing exercises in the texts generally follow the reading, speaking and listening activities and build upon the previous exercises. The writing exercises are controlled either through format and structure (filling in words, using forms, etc.), or a model is provided with the exercise. Students should be encouraged to draw freely from the model when writing.

The authors also recommend using pre-writing strategies such as brain-storming for ideas and vocabulary, reviewing the reading with a focus on finding specific vocabulary or grammatical structures, group discussion about the writing task, and having the instructor or other class members create a model. The writing assignment may be done as an individual, partner, or group activity.

Using Math and Graphs

The *Workskills* texts include a basic math and graphical skills component in each unit. These exercises were designed to enhance basic skills and meet basic job and personal math needs for the student. The units focus on problems that students will encounter either at work or in their daily lives. Successful completion of all these exercises should prepare students for most basic uses of math in the workplace. Supplemental practice and additional exercises may be necessary for students with limited mathematical background or those who will need a higher level of proficiency on their jobs.

Acknowledgments

We wish to thank the following people:

Elizabeth Minicz
Roseanne Mendoza
Sheila McMillen
Anne Riddick
Rosemary Palicki
Marilyn Antonik

We are also grateful to our students at

Barrett Bindery
C-Line Office Products
College of DuPage
Filtran
Johnson & Quin
Navistar International
Oakton Community College
Panek Precision
Schwake Stone Co.
Triton College

A special thanks to everyone who helped me obtain authentic materials for my research.—S.Q.

This book is dedicated to my family—Mario, Allison, Jimmy and to the memory of a special friend—Holly.

UNIT 1   *Company Policies*

Before You Read
(making predictions, relating experiences to reading, establishing prior knowledge)

Credit: Charles Gupton/UNIPHOTO

Talk about this picture with a partner.

Write your answers on the lines.

1. What happened to this man?_____

    _____

2. How do you think it happened? _____

    _____

3. Can he work? _____

    _____

4. What do you think will happen if he can't work? _____

    _____

5. What is a *leave of absence?* _____

    _____

Reading About Work

Antonio's Bad Break

Yesterday was Sunday, so Antonio didn't go to work. He and some of his friends decided to play a game of soccer in the afternoon. Antonio was excited and happy because he was playing a good game. He even helped to make one of his team's goals. The score was 3–1. Antonio's team was winning, but then something terrible happened! Antonio and his friend Rico were both trying to get the ball, when they crashed into one another. Antonio fell on his arm. He knew right away that something was wrong because his arm hurt so much.

Antonio lay on the field. He couldn't get up. His friends ran over to help him. They decided to take him to the emergency room at the hospital. When they arrived at the emergency room, it was very crowded. Antonio had to wait half an hour before a doctor looked at his arm and took X-rays. Antonio waited anxiously for the results of the X-rays.

A nurse told him that his arm was broken. The doctor put a cast on it. He told Antonio that it was necessary to keep his arm in the cast and immobile for four weeks.

Antonio was very upset. He started to think about his job. He liked his job in the factory, where he had started to work as a packer only two months ago. And now his arm was in a cast! How could he work? What would happen?

On Monday morning, Antonio called his boss and told him about the accident. The doctor said that he could not work for a month.

What do you think Antonio's boss said to him?

Understanding New Words

(expanding vocabulary, understanding new words through context)

Read these sentences with a partner. Decide together if *a* or *b* has the same meaning as the sentence. Circle *a* or *b*.

1. The <u>score</u> was 3–1.

   (a.) One team had 3 points. The other team had 1 point.

   b. This is a math problem. The answer is 2.

2. Antonio and his friend Rico <u>crashed into</u> each other.

   a. They ran into each other very hard.

   b. They ran past each other.

3. Antonio knew <u>right away</u> that something was wrong.

   a. He found out later that something was wrong.

   b. He found out immediately that something was wrong.

4. The emergency room was very <u>crowded</u>.

   a. The emergency room was very noisy.

   b. There were many people in the emergency room.

5. Antonio waited <u>anxiously</u>.

   a. He was very nervous and worried.

   b. He was very relaxed and calm.

6. The doctor put a <u>cast</u> on Antonio's arm.

   a. The doctor put on a special covering to help fix Antonio's broken bone.

   b. The doctor put a jacket on Antonio's arm.

7. It was necessary to keep his arm <u>immobile</u>.

   a. He needed to exercise his arm.

   b. He could not move his arm.

8. Antonio was very <u>upset</u>.

   a. He was very unhappy and angry.

   b. He was very surprised.

9. He liked his job as a <u>packer</u>.

   a. He liked his job inspecting products.

   b. He liked his job putting products in boxes.

Understanding the Reading

Activity 1 *(identifying details, checking literal comprehension)*

Read these sentences with a partner. Decide together if they are *true* or *false.* Then write *true* or *false* on the line.

_____false_____ 1. Antonio works on Sunday.

_____ 2. Antonio and his friends were playing football.

_____ 3. Antonio and Rico had an accident.

_____ 4. Antonio hurt his leg.

_____ 5. A nurse took X-rays of his arm.

_____ 6. Antonio's arm was broken.

_____ 7. Antonio had to wear a cast for four weeks.

_____ 8. Antonio had his job for a long time.

_____ 9. Antonio couldn't work for two months.

Activity 2 *(sequencing events in chronological order)*

Think about the story. Put the sentences in the order in which they happened. Put number *1* next to what happened first, number *2* next to what happened second, and so on.

_____ Antonio fell on his arm.

_____1_____ Antonio and his friends decided to play soccer.

_____ The doctor took X-rays.

_____ Antonio called his boss.

_____ Antonio and Rico crashed into one another.

_____ The doctor put a cast on Antonio's arm.

_____ Antonio waited half an hour.

_____ Antonio's friends took him to the emergency room.

Activity 3 *(summarizing the story)*

Write the sentences from Activity 2 in the correct order. When you finish, you will have a summary of the story.

Antonio and his friends decided to play soccer.

_____

_____

_____

_____

_____

Discussing

Activity 1 *(making judgments, making predictions)*

Imagine that the people in these stories work for your company. Read each story with a partner. In each case, what is your company's policy about taking time off?

1. Tran is very sick. He has a bad cold and a fever. He plans to go to the doctor this afternoon. He knows that he will miss a few days of work. How many times does he need to call his boss? Only the first day that he is sick? Or every day that he is sick? Does he need a note from his doctor?

2. Mohammad wants to celebrate Eid Ul Akber. This is a religious holiday in his country, but it is not a holiday in the United States. He wants to take off one day of work. Can he do this?

3. Rosalia is pregnant. She will have her baby in about four weeks. She wants to stay at home as long as possible with her new baby. How long can she stay with her new baby before she has to go back to work?

4. Last night, Krystyna received a phone call from her mother in Poland. Her father is very sick, and he wants Krystyna to visit him. Krystyna has not visited her family for five years, so she wants to go. She wants to stay in Poland for two weeks. What can she do?

5. José's grandmother died in Mexico. He wants to attend the funeral. He needs to leave for Mexico tomorrow. What does José need to do?

6. Lien's daughter is very sick. She needs to have an operation, and Lien wants to be with her daughter when she goes to the hospital. Lien wants to take off ten days of work to be with her daughter. What is the company policy?

Activity 2 *(using creative thinking to complete a conversation)*

Finish the conversation. It is Monday morning, and Josef is calling his supervisor because he is sick.

MR. CURTIS: Good morning. Ace Tool Company. Mr. Curtis speaking.

JOSEF: _____

MR. CURTIS: I'm sorry that you're sick, Josef. What's the problem?

JOSEF: _____

MR. CURTIS: When do you think that you can come back to work?

JOSEF: _____

MR. CURTIS: Well, if you don't come to work tomorrow, you need to call me again. I hope that you can come back tomorrow. We need you to operate your machine. Take care of yourself.

Writing
(writing explanations regarding an emergency at work)

Imagine this situation: You are at work and you receive a phone call from your husband (or wife). There is an emergency at home, and you need to leave your job immediately. Your boss is on break, and you can't find him or her. Read the model below, and then write a note to your boss explaining why you need to go home.

April 10

Dear Mr. Fisher,

I received a phone call from my wife. There is an emergency at my house.

It is raining very hard, and there is a lot of water in my basement. I need to

go home now at 2:00.

Tran

_____

_____

_____

_____

Reading at Work

Understanding New Words
(expanding vocabulary, understanding new words through context)

Read the sentences below. Find and circle the underlined words in the reading that follows.

1. An <u>hourly rated employee</u> earns money each hour that he or she works. The minimum wage of an <u>hourly rated employee</u> is $4.25 per hour.
2. Martha started to work for Excel Corporation in 1986. In 1991, she completed five years' <u>continuous</u> service.
3. After Penpank completes one year at Excel Corporation, she will be <u>eligible</u> for one week of vacation. She can have one week of vacation.
4. A <u>calendar year</u> is a 12-month period starting from an employee's first day of work.
5. Barbara's <u>anniversary date</u> at Excel Corporation is October 15th of each year. October 15th is the date that she started to work at Excel Corporation.

Read the following excerpt from the policy manual of the Excel Corporation.

VACATION POLICY OF EXCEL CORPORATION

Section 1. The vacation year will be from January 1 to December 31. Each hourly rated employee who has completed one (or more) years of continuous service with the Company shall receive the following vacation time:

Years of Continuous Service	Amount of Vacation
One	One week
Four or more	Two weeks
Nine or more	Three weeks

Explanation:
An employee shall not be eligible for any vacation until he has completed one full year of continuous service. An employee becomes eligible for additional vacation time during the calendar year in which his anniversary date falls.

Understanding the Reading

Activity 1 *(applying information from the reading)*

Read the following situations. Fill in the blanks according to the vacation policy of Excel Corporation.

1. An employee cannot take a vacation until he or she has _____one_____ year(s) of continuous service at Excel Corporation.

2. An employee who has worked at this company continuously from March 1, 1989, to March 1, 1991, has _____ week(s) of vacation time.

3. An employee who has seven years of continuous service will receive _____ week(s) of vacation time.

4. If an employee starts to work for Excel Corporation in July 1986, he is eligible for three weeks of vacation in July _____.

Activity 2: What about your company? *(relating reading to company policy)*

Discuss the following questions in groups. Then share your answers with the class.

1. How long do you need to work for your company before you are eligible for vacation time?
2. When does your vacation time increase from one week to two weeks? From two weeks to three weeks? When does it increase to more than three weeks?
3. You want to take your vacation from August 7th to August 21st. How do you arrange your vacation time with your supervisor?

Listening
(listening for specific information and problem solving)

   Mrs. Smith from Personnel is talking to Tom, the supervisor of the cookie division at the Sweet Tooth Bakery. Many employees are absent because they are sick with the flu.

1. Listen to the conversation on the tape. Decide which employees are absent. Check (✔) *At Work* or *Absent* for each employee.
2. You need to make new crews. On the line *Additional Experience*, write another job that the person can do.

	Dough Mixer	Machine Operator	Inspector	Packer	At Work	Absent	Additional Experience
José Gomez	X						
Tyree Washington		X					
Ana Roselli			X				
Rosa Garcia				X			
John Ring	X						
Luis Gonzalez		X					
Andrej Fedor				X			
Teresa Witkowski			X				
Liu Chen	X						
Helga Fromm		X					
Diane Star				X			
Marie Andropoulos			X				

3. In groups, compare your information. Then use the information from the chart to make *two* crews that can bake cookies at the Sweet Tooth Bakery today.

Crew 1

Dough Mixer _____

Machine Operator _____

Inspector _____

Packer _____

Crew 2

Dough Mixer _____

Machine Operator _____

Inspector _____

Packer _____

Reading Graphs

Activity 1 *(reading and interpreting a line graph)*

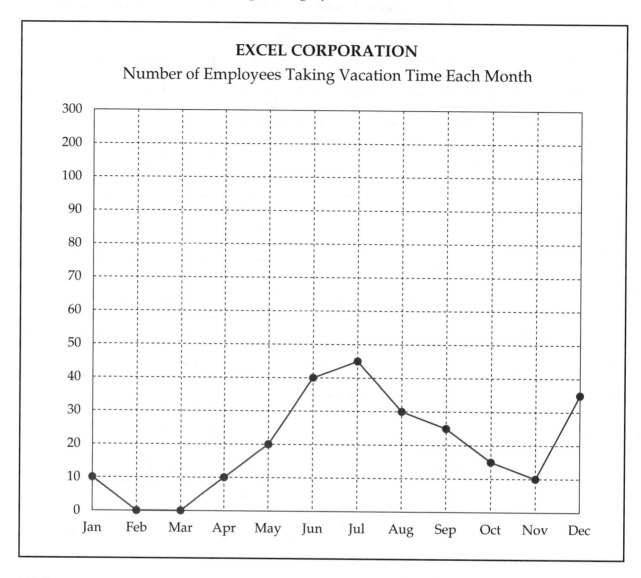

EXCEL CORPORATION

Number of Employees Taking Vacation Time Each Month

With a partner, look at the graph of vacation time. Answer the following questions.

1. How many employees take vacation in January? _____10_____

2. How many employees take vacation in July? _____
    In October? _____

3. In which month(s) do the fewest employees take vacation? _____

4. What is the peak month for vacations? _____

5. Do more people take vacations in June or in August? _____

6. What is the peak month for vacations at your company? _____

Activity 2 *(plotting and interpreting information on a line graph)*

Below is a list of how many units are produced each month at the Excel Corporation. Work with a partner. Plot this information on the graph.

January	12,000 units	July	9,750 units
February	13,000 units	August	10,500 units
March	13,500 units	September	10,750 units
April	11,750 units	October	12,000 units
May	11,250 units	November	12,250 units
June	10,000 units	December	10,250 units

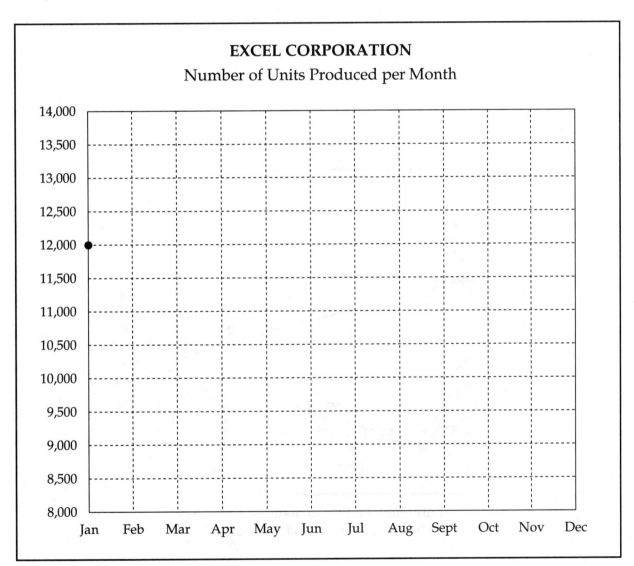

EXCEL CORPORATION

Number of Units Produced per Month

With your partner, look at your production graph. Answer the following questions:

1. In which month(s) is production highest?_____

2. In which month(s) is production lowest? _____

3. Are more units produced in April or in September? _____

Now compare the *two* graphs of the Excel Corporation on pages 10 and 11.

4.   What happens to production in July when 45 people take vacation? _____

_____

5.   What happens to production in March when no one takes vacation? _____

_____

6.   What conclusion can you draw about vacations and production levels?

_____

"... and now I'd like to discuss new ways
to fight our absenteeism problem."

Before You Read
(making predictions, relating experiences to reading, establishing prior knowledge)

Credit: Irene Springer

Talk about this photograph with a partner.

Write your answers on the line.

1. What kind of store is this? _____

2. What does the sign say? _____

3. What other ways can you find out about sales in stores? _____

   _____

4. What do you buy on sale? _____

5. What problems do you have when you try to buy things on sale?

   _____

Reading About Work

The Big Sale

Olena works at Doyle's, a large department store. She works in the electronics department, where people can buy televisions, computers, radios, and VCRs. Olena is a salesperson. Her job is to answer customers' questions about products and to operate the cash register. She has an extra duty when Doyle's has a sale. It is her job to put up sale signs in the electronics department.

Last Friday night, just before the store closed, Mrs. Gomez called Olena to her office. Mrs. Gomez is Olena's supervisor. She told Olena that, on Saturday, Doyle's was going to have a special sale on VCRs and cassette tapes. Mrs. Gomez told Olena to put up sale signs. All VCRs were 25% off the regular price. All movies on tapes were 20% off, and all blank tapes were 50% off.

Olena was not listening carefully to Mrs. Gomez. She was in a hurry to leave the store. Doyle's closes at 9:30 on Friday nights, and Olena was going to meet some friends at 10:00. She was thinking about seeing her friends at the Pizza House. She wasn't thinking about her job.

Olena couldn't put up the sale signs until the store closed. At about 9:40, she finished her other duties. Then she picked up the signs. She asked herself, "Now, what did Mrs. Gomez want me to do? I don't remember exactly what she said, but I have only 20 minutes to get to the Pizza House. I need to hurry." Olena quickly put the signs around the department:

50% off—in VCR section

25% off—on tables of blank tapes

20% off—on tables of movies

Doyle's opened at 9:00 the next morning. Mrs. Gomez arrived at 10:30. She was very surprised. A lot of people were buying VCRs, but only a few customers were buying tapes. Then she saw the sale sign in the VCR section: 50% off. She was very angry. She asked another salesperson, "Where's Olena?"

Understanding New Words

(expanding vocabulary, understanding new words through context)

Read these sentences with a partner. Decide together if *a* or *b* describes the underlined words. Circle *a* or *b*.

1. Olena has an extra <u>duty</u> when Doyle's has a sale.

   a. helper
   (b.) responsibility or job

2. Last Friday night, <u>just before the store closed</u>, Mrs. Gomez called Olena to her office.

   a. exactly when the store closed
   b. a few minutes before the store closed

3. Doyle's was going to have a special sale on VCRs and <u>cassette tapes</u>.

   a. rectangular plastic boxes to insert in a VCR
   b. radios

4. All <u>movies</u> on tapes were 20% off.

   a. televisions
   b. films

5. All <u>blank</u> tapes were 50% off.

   a. tapes with nothing on them
   b. tapes with a film on them

6. <u>Olena was in a hurry to leave the store.</u>

   a. She wanted to leave the store at 10:00.
   b. She wanted to leave the store quickly.

Understanding the Reading

(identifying details, checking literal and inferential comprehension)

Read these sentences with a partner. Decide together if they are *true* or *false*. Then write *true* or *false* on the line.

_____*true*_____ 1. Olena works in a department store.

_____ 2. Olena works in the men's department.

_____ 3. One of Olena's duties is to operate the cash register.

_____ 4. Mrs. Gomez is Olena's supervisor.

_____ 5. Last Friday night, Olena carefully put up the sale signs in the electronics department.

_____ 6. Mrs. Gomez wanted Olena to put the 20%-off sign on the table of movie tapes.

_____ 7. On Saturday morning, the customers were buying a lot of tapes.

_____ 8. Mrs. Gomez was angry with the customers.

_____ 9. Olena followed all of Mrs. Gomez's directions.

Discussing

Activity 1: Ordering *(sequencing actions)*

We give directions or follow instructions every day, and it is important to do things in the *proper order.* Think about starting a car. The correct order is:

1. Insert key in ignition.
2. Turn key.
3. Put foot on brake.
4. Put car in "drive."
5. Remove foot from brake.
6. Put foot on accelerator.
7. Drive.

Some of the activities that you do on break at work—making coffee, using a pay telephone, or buying coffee from a vending machine require following instructions in a specific order.

Read the following activities with a partner. Decide in which order you do them. Put number *1* next to what you do first, number *2* next to what you do second, and so on. The first exercise is started for you.

Making drip coffee

_____ Put filter holder into coffeemaker.

_____ Fill coffeepot with water.

_____ Turn on power.

_____ Put empty coffeepot on hot plate.

_____2_____ Measure coffee.

_____ Coffee is ready when coffeepot is full.

_____ Pour water from coffeepot into coffeemaker.

_____1_____ Put filter into filter holder.

_____ Put coffee into filter.

Using a pay telephone

_____ Listen for dial tone.

_____ Punch in telephone number.

_____ Phone will ring.

_____ Insert money.

_____ Pick up receiver.

Using a vending machine—buying coffee (35 cents)

_____ Make sure coffee cup is straight when it comes down.

_____ Press down and hold buttons for "extra cream" and "extra sugar."

_____ Insert money (2 quarters).

_____ Wait for change.

_____ Select "coffee with cream and sugar."

_____ Release buttons when cup is full.

Activity 2: Questions to think about and discuss *(discussing and reporting information to class, relating reading to work experiences)*

Talk about these questions in groups. Then report back to the class.

1. Think about Olena's situation.

    a. What did she do wrong?

    b. What happened when she didn't follow instructions?

    c. If she is in the same situation again, what does she need to do differently?

2. When do you follow instructions at work?

3. What instructions do you follow?

4. When do you give directions at work?

5. What directions do you give?

6. Why is it important to give directions clearly and to follow instructions carefully?

Reading at Work

Understanding New Words
(expanding vocabulary, understanding new words through context, labeling a picture)

Study the following picture of a photocopy machine. Using the numbers, identify the parts listed here. Then write the new words on the lines in the picture. The first one is written for you.

1. Power Switch
2. Copyboard Cover
3. Upper Cassette
4. Lower Cassette
5. Control Panel

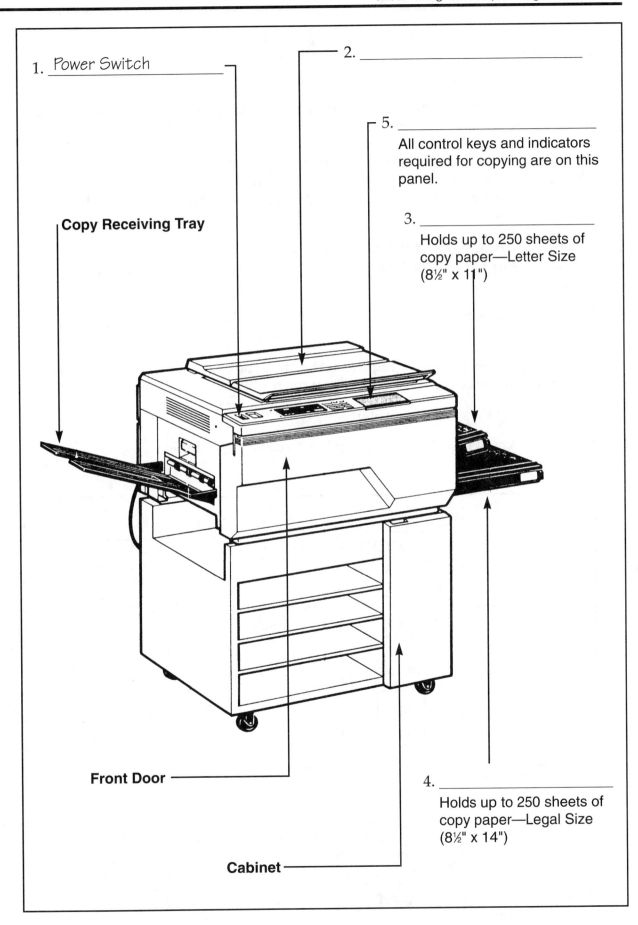

1. Power Switch

2. _____

5. _____

All control keys and indicators required for copying are on this panel.

3. _____

Holds up to 250 sheets of copy paper—Letter Size (8½" x 11")

Copy Receiving Tray

Front Door _____

4. _____

Holds up to 250 sheets of copy paper—Legal Size (8½" x 14")

Cabinet _____

Understanding the Reading

Activity 1: Matching *(checking literal comprehension, reading and applying information)*

Read the following instructions for operating a photocopy machine. Then match the pictures with the correct description.

1. **Turning the power on:** Power is on when the power switch is on "I."
    •When the power switch is turned on, a red light tells the operator to wait. After approximately 90 seconds, the light turns green. You can then begin making copies.

2. **Position the original:** Lift the copyboard cover. Put the original copy face down in the upper left corner of the copyboard glass. Carefully lower the copyboard cover.

3. **Select the copy paper:** Press the Cassette Selection key to select the upper or lower cassette.

4. **Enter the number of copies required:** Use the Input Keyboard to enter the required number of copies (1–99). Check the number on the Control Panel.

5. **Start copying:** Press the Copy Start key ▮.

6. **Clear/Stop key:** Press the Clear/Stop key to clear the number of copies or to stop copying.

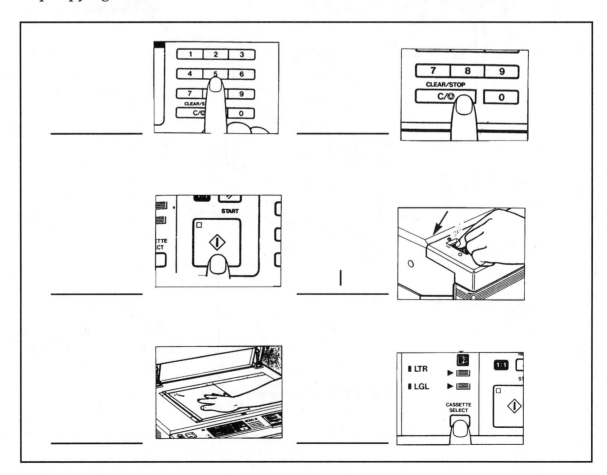

Activity 2: True/False *(identifying details, checking literal and inferential comprehension)*

Read these sentences about the photocopy machine with a partner. Decide together if they are *true* or *false*. Then write *true* or *false* on the line. Then CORRECT the false sentences.

_____false_____ 1. You can make copies if the light is ~~red~~. *green*

_____ 2. You put the original face up on the copyboard glass.

_____ 3. You put the original in the upper left corner.

_____ 4. The upper and lower cassettes contain the copy paper.

_____ 5. You can make more than 99 copies at one time on this machine.

_____ 6. You press the Start key to turn on the power.

_____ 7. You press the Clear/Stop key if you want to stop making copies.

Listening
(listening for specific information, problem solving)

Miss McCormick, the assistant manager at Doyle's, is sick today. She didn't finish filling out the schedule for breaks before she left yesterday. This morning she called the store to leave instructions for taking breaks. Listen to the instructions and finish the schedule.

	Jewelry	Men's Furnishings	Housewares	Domestics	Morning Break	Afternoon Break
Letty	X					
George		X				
Marta	X					
Sam		X				
Fred			X			
Sylvia			X			
Izabella				X		
Brenda				X		

Understanding a Flow Chart

Activity 1: The cash register *(discussing and interpreting a diagram of a cash register)*

The salespeople at Doyle's need to follow instructions to operate a cash register. Look at the picture below of a cash register, and answer the questions.

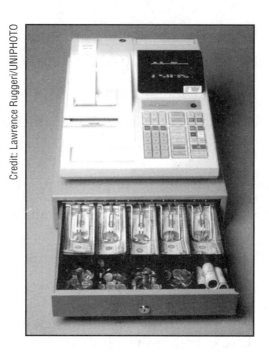

Credit: Lawrence Ruggeri/UNIPHOTO

1.   Where is the key that opens the register?

2.   Where are the number keys?

3.   In what order are the numbers?

4.   Where is the *Enter key*?

5.   Where is the *Total key*?

6.   Where is the *cash register window*?

Activity 2: The flow chart *(reading about and interpreting a flow chart)*

There are many different ways to explain instructions. We can *tell* our instructions to another person, or we can *write* our instructions. We can also *show* our instructions on a flow-chart—a *picture* of our instructions.

Below are step-by-step instructions to turn on and operate a cash register at Doyle's. Read the explanation.

1. In the morning when the store opens, Mrs. Gomez opens the cash register in the electronics department with a <u>key</u>.

2. Then Mrs. Gomez enters the <u>store code</u> (2 numbers or 2 digits). For Doyle's, the store code is <u>53</u>.

3. Each employee has an <u>employee code</u> (3 digits). Mrs. Gomez's code is <u>147</u>, so she enters the number 147.

4. Then Mrs. Gomez needs to enter the <u>date</u> (2 digits for the month, 2 digits for the day, and 2 digits for the year). If the date is September 4, 1993, Mrs. Gomez will enter <u>09 04 93</u>. Now she is ready for customers.

5. When a customer buys something, Mrs. Gomez enters the <u>sku number</u> (6 digits) from the price tag. A <u>sku number</u> looks like this: <u>019822</u>.

6. Next, Mrs. Gomez presses the <u>Enter key</u>.

7. Then the price ($5.99) shows on the <u>cash register window</u>.

8. Next, Mrs. Gomez presses the <u>Enter key</u> again.

9. If the customer is buying more than one item, Mrs. Gomez repeats steps 5, 6, 7 and 8 again.

10. After Mrs. Gomez enters everything that the customer wants to buy, she presses the <u>Total key</u> for the total price including tax.

A flow chart or picture of the instructions may help you to understand better how to operate a cash register. Look at the two flow charts that follow. The flow chart on the left shows the general instructions for operating a cash register. The flow chart on the right shows how Mrs. Gomez operates the cash register in the electronics department at Doyle's.

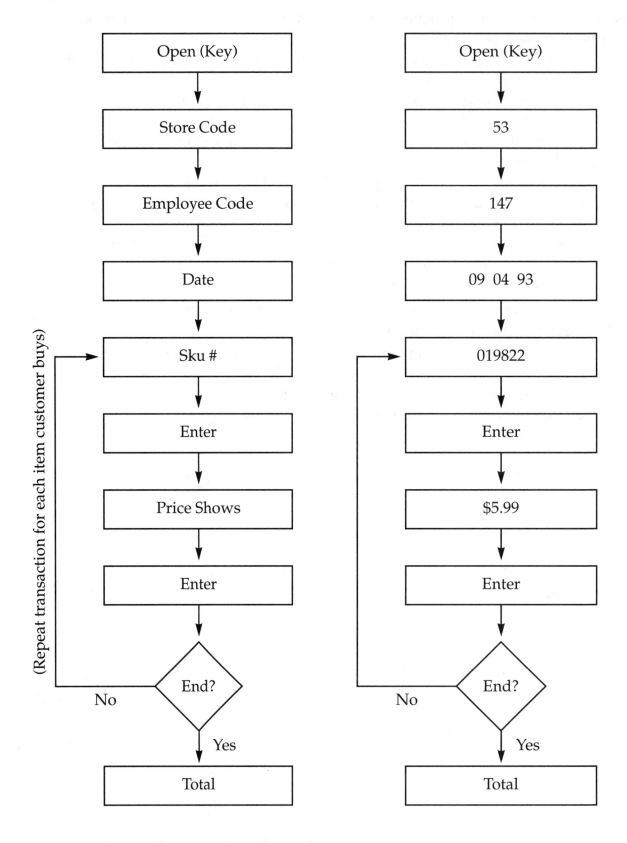

Activity 3: Filling in a flow chart *(synthesizing information to fill in a flow chart)*

With a partner, use the information below to fill in the flow chart.

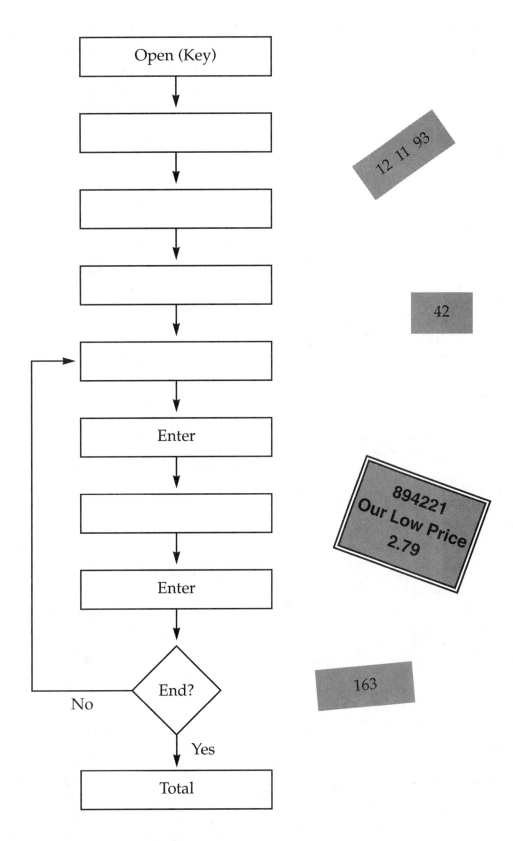

Writing

Activity 1: Writing a flow chart (*writing directions in flow chart form*)

Following are instructions for operating a photocopy machine. Complete the flow chart with a partner. Put the instructions on the right in the correct places on the flow chart on the left. (Remember that the diamond-shaped box means that you have to make a decision. Look at the question. If you answer *yes*, continue down. If you answer *no*, you need to make a "loop" to change the incorrect number of copies.)

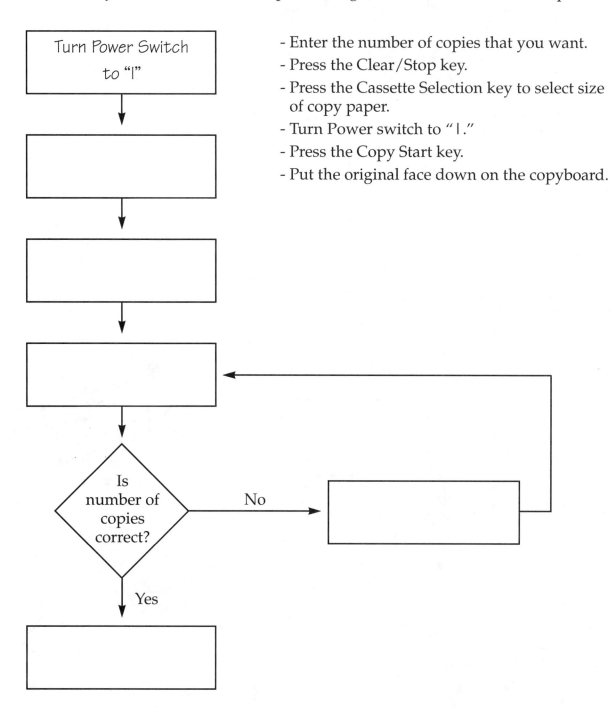

- Enter the number of copies that you want.
- Press the Clear/Stop key.
- Press the Cassette Selection key to select size of copy paper.
- Turn Power switch to "I."
- Press the Copy Start key.
- Put the original face down on the copyboard.

Activity 2: Signs *(identifying signs)*

Look around at work. Copy all the signs that give directions.

No Smoking

_____   _____

_____   _____

_____   _____

_____   _____

"What does the flashing red light mean?"

UNIT 3 *Safety*

Talk about this picture with a partner.

Write your answers on the lines.

1. Where are these workers? _____

2. What are they doing? _____

3. Which work conditions are not safe? _____

   Why not? _____

   _____

4. What can the company do to make the conditions safe? _____

   _____

5. What are some safety rules where you work? _____

   _____

Reading About Work

Safety, Safety, Safety

It was the first day back to work after Excel Corporation's week-long shut down. Penpank and Marcella were walking to the employee cafeteria. Penpank said, "I don't understand why we're having another safety meeting. We just had a meeting after Christmas."

Marcella explained, "You started to work here only two months ago, Penpank. You'll see that this company does many things to promote safety. Every week, we receive safety bulletins when we come into the factory. We have monthly safety meetings where we can discuss any safety problems we have. We also have safety meetings when there are accidents in the factory and after a company shut down. You see, Excel doesn't want us to forget safety rules. And, each month, there is a special safety award for the safest department."

As the women entered the cafeteria, the foreman was telling everyone to sit down. "Department 36, the safety meeting will begin in two minutes." Marcella and Penpank sat down. Marcella told Penpank, "At these meetings, we usually see a safety film. Sometimes the films are about operating machines safely or about working with hazardous chemicals. These films help us to be very alert for dangers on the job. Sometimes we think that we know our job very well—but if we are careless for one second, something bad can happen."

The foreman started the meeting with good news. "Department 36, you won the safety award for this month—no accidents! Congratulations! Free coffee and soft drinks for everyone in Department 36 for the next 24 hours! Now, let's discuss the problems that you had last month . . ."

Penpank whispered to Marcella, "I'm glad that I work in Department 36. It's nice to win the award and have free coffee, but it's even nicer to work in a very safe department!"

Understanding New Words

(expanding vocabulary, understanding new words through context)

Read these pairs of sentences with a partner. Decide if the meaning of the sentences is the same or different. Circle *Same* or *Different*.

1. Sometimes a company has a shut down when there is not much work.
   Sometimes a company gives workers a vacation with no pay when there is not much work.

   Same   Different

2. This company does many things to promote safety.
   This company does many things to make safety a very important idea.

   Same   Different

3. We receive safety bulletins when we come into the factory.
   We receive papers with safety information when we come into the factory.

   Same   Different

4. We see films about working with hazardous chemicals.
   We see films about working with safe chemicals.

   Same   Different

5. These films help us to be alert for dangers on the job.
   These films help us to look for dangers on the job.

   Same   Different

6. If we are careless for one second, something bad can happen.
   If we don't pay attention for one second, something bad can happen.

   Same   Different

7. Penpank whispered to Marcella.
   Penpank talked loudly to Marcella.

   Same   Different

Understanding the Reading

Activity 1 *(identifying specific details, checking literal comprehension)*

Read these sentences with a partner. One word in each sentence is not correct. Decide which word is wrong, and write the correct sentence on the line below.

1. It was the first day back to work after Excel Corporation's ~~month~~-long *week* shut down.

   It was the first day back to work after Excel Corporation's week-long

   shut down.

2. Penpank started to work at Excel Corporation three months ago.

   _____

3. The employees have weekly safety meetings.

   _____

4. At the safety meetings, the workers can talk about any personal problems that they have.

_____

_____

5. If workers are careful for one second, something bad can happen.

_____

6. The foreman started the meeting with bad news.

_____

7. Penpank is sad that she works in Department 36.

_____

Activity 2 *(understanding the main idea)*

On the lines below, write the answers to the questions.

1. What are four (4) ways that Excel Corporation promotes safety?

_____

_____

_____

_____

2. Why does Excel Corporation promote safety in the factory?

_____

_____

Discussing

Activity 1: Check your safety knowledge *(making predictions)*

Read the following sentences with a partner. Circle the answer that you think is correct.

1. In the United States each year, accidents kill

    a. 11 people every hour
    b. 2 people every hour
    c. 9 people every hour

2. In this country each year, accidents injure one person

    a. every 30 seconds
    b. every 10 seconds
    c. every 4 seconds

3. In the U.S. every year, accidents cost the people almost

    a. $90 million ($90,000,000)
    b. $90 billion ($90,000,000,000)
    c. $20 billion ($20,000,000,000)

4. In this country, accidents are the _____ for all people between the ages of 1 and 38.

    a. #1 reason for death
    b. #2 reason for death
    c. #3 reason for death

5. Every year, *work* accidents kill more than

    a. 2,000 people
    b. 11,000 people
    c. 20,000 people

6. Each year, work accidents disable (a person's body doesn't work properly) about

    a. 500,000 people
    b. 1,000,000 people
    c. 2,000,000 people

7. Every year, work accidents cost more than _____ in medical fees, sick pay, and replacement wages (money to pay another worker).

    a. $35 billion ($35,000,000,000)
    b. $10 billion ($10,000,000,000)
    c. $20 million ($20,000,000)

Answers for *Discussing, Activity 1: (Check your safety knowledge.)*
  1. a 2. c 3. b 4. a 5. b 6. c 7. a

Activity 2: Signs *(completing safety signs)*

With a partner, look at the signs on this page. Use the words on the right to complete the signs. The first one is done for you.

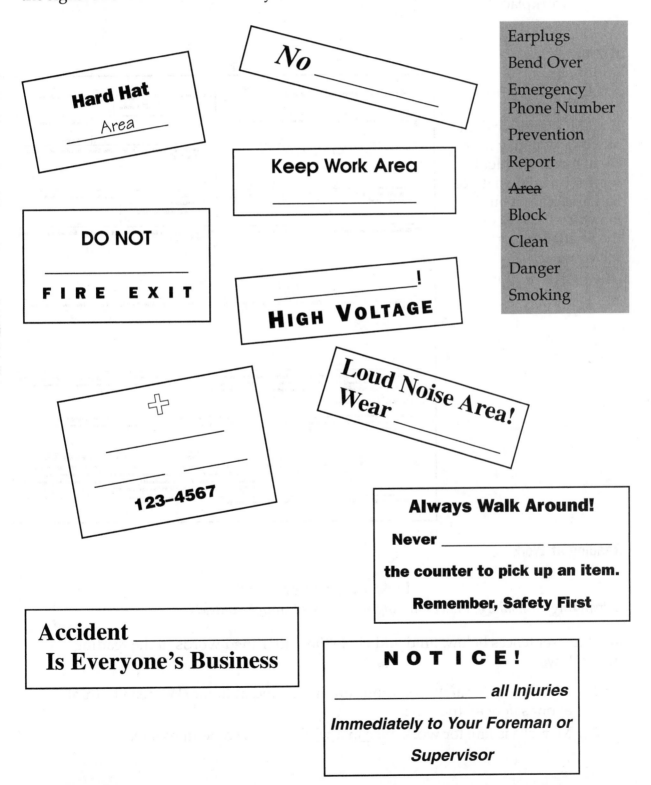

Earplugs
Bend Over
Emergency Phone Number
Prevention
Report
~~Area~~
Block
Clean
Danger
Smoking

Hard Hat
Area

No _____

Keep Work Area
_____

DO NOT
_____
FIRE EXIT

_____!
HIGH VOLTAGE

☩
_____
__ __
123-4567

Loud Noise Area!
Wear _____

Always Walk Around!
Never _____ _____
the counter to pick up an item.
Remember, Safety First

Accident _____
Is Everyone's Business

NOTICE!
_____ all Injuries
Immediately to Your Foreman or
Supervisor

Activity 3: Safety signs *(recognizing and discussing reasons for safety signs)*

In groups, talk about these questions:

1. Which of the signs from Activity 2 are at your workplace? What other safety signs are at your workplace? Why are those signs there?

2. Look at *Writing, Activity 2* from Unit 2 on page 27. Which of the directions that you wrote down are safety signs? Why are they important at your workplace?

Writing

(filling out an accident report form)

If you have an accident at work, you may need to fill out an accident report. Imagine that you had an accident on the job yesterday. Fill out the accident report for yourself.

1. Name of Injured Employee (Last, first, middle)		2. Date of Birth	3. ☐ Male ☐ Female	4. Social Security Number
5. Employee's Home Mailing Address (no., street, city, state, zip code)				6. Home Telephone Area Code: Number:
7. Name and Address of Employing Agency		8. Place Where Injury Occurred (e.g., 2nd floor, Main Post Office Bldg., 12th & Pine)		
9. Date and Hour of Injury (mo., day, year) ☐ AM ☐ PM	10. Date of This Notice. (mo., day, year)	11. Dependents Wife/Husband ☐ Children/Under 18 Years Old ☐		12. Employee's Occupation
13. Cause of Injury (Describe how and why the injury occurred)		14. Nature of Injury (Identify the part of the body injured, e.g., fractured left leg, etc.)		

15. If This Notice and Claim Was Not Filed With The Employing Agency Within Two Working Days After The Injury, Explain The Reason For The Delay.

16. I certify, under penalty of law, that the injury described above was sustained in performance of duty as an employee of the United States Government and that it was not caused by my willful misconduct, intent to injure myself or another person, nor by my intoxication. I hereby claim medical treatment, if needed, and the following, as checked below, while disabled for work:

☐ a. Sick and/or Annual leave.

☐ b. Continuation of regular pay not to exceed 45 days and compensation for wage loss if disability for work continues beyond 45 days (If my claim is denied, I understand that the continuation of my regular pay shall be charged to sick or annual leave, or be deemed an overpayment within the meaning of 5 USC 5584).

Signature of Employee or Person Acting on His/Her Behalf

PENALTY PROVISION: Any person who knowingly makes any false statement, misrepresentation, concealment of fact, or any other act of fraud to obtain compensation as provided by the FECA or who knowingly accepts compensation to which that person is not entitled is subject to felony criminal prosecution and may, under appropriate U.S. Criminal Code provisions, be punished by a fine of not more than $10,000 or imprisonment for not more than five years, or both.

17. Statement of Witness (Describe what you saw, heard or know about this injury)

Reading at Work

Understanding New Words

(expanding vocabulary, understanding new words through context)

Read the sentences below. Find and circle the underlined words in the reading that follows.

1. We need to be safety <u>conscious</u> on the job and at home. We need to think about safety all the time.

2. Marcella is late for work <u>once in a while</u>. She is sometimes late.

3. Mrs. Garcia <u>posted</u> the job announcement yesterday. She put it on the wall by the vending machines.

4. If you work with machinery, you need to take some <u>precautions</u>. You can't wear jewelry or very loose clothing, and you need to tie back your long hair.

5. English classes are <u>available</u> at some workplaces. For example, you can take classes at this workplace.

6. Workers also <u>take care of</u> cleaning up their work areas. They are responsible for cleaning up their work areas.

Understanding the Reading

(identifying personal safety practices)

Read the following "quiz" about safety and circle the answers that describe you best.

WHAT'S YOUR SAFETY SCORE?

Safe Habits Are Easy To Learn

We all try to be safety conscious, but at times we find excuses for not acting safely, both on and off the job. This quick "quiz" can help you identify some common safety practices, and may help you find areas that you can improve. Take a few minutes to find out your safety score. (Circle the answer that you think best describes your own practices.)

Safe Practices

1. I read labels before I use chemicals.
    usually   once in a while   never

2. When I start a new job, I ask questions so I understand how to do my job.
    usually   once in a while   never

3. I come to work well-rested and awake.
    usually   once in a while   never

4. Emergency police, medical, and fire numbers are posted where everyone can find them.
    yes   no

Safe Conditions

5. I know the hazards of my job, and I don't begin until I take all necessary precautions.
    usually   once in a while   never

6. I inspect the area and machines I'm responsible for.
    usually   once in a while   never

7. When the proper safety equipment is not available, I tell my supervisor right away.
    usually   once in a while   never

8. When I see a condition that is dangerous, I take care of it or tell my supervisor right away.
    usually   once in a while   never

Safe Attitudes

9. When I'm angry, I take a "time out" before going back to a possibly dangerous task.
    usually   once in a while   never

10. I'm careful to put out matches, cigarettes, or fires completely.
    usually   once in a while   never

11. When I take a safety class, I ask questions and pay attention.
    usually   once in a while   never

12. I relax without alcohol or drugs.
    usually   once in a while   never

SCORING   Give yourself 3 points for each "usually" or "yes," 2 points for each "once in a while," and 1 point for each "never" or "no."
Over 20   *Excellent.* Excellent attitude, habits, and a bright, safe future.
16–20   *Good.* Select 5 areas for improvement and try to change your "once in a whiles" to "usually."
12–15   *Lucky.* You're lucky if you've never been in an accident. Work on changing your "once in a whiles" or "nevers" to "usually."
Under 12   *Time Bomb.* You are an accident waiting to happen. Better start working on 5 dangerous habits today!

Listening
(listening for specific information)

Henry Chin and Anthony Carter are starting their first day of work at the ABC Steel Company. Henry is a painter and Anthony is an electrician. Mr. Gray, the safety manager, is talking to them about the safety equipment that they each need for their jobs.

Look at the items in each man's locker below. Listen to the tape and circle the equipment that each man needs.

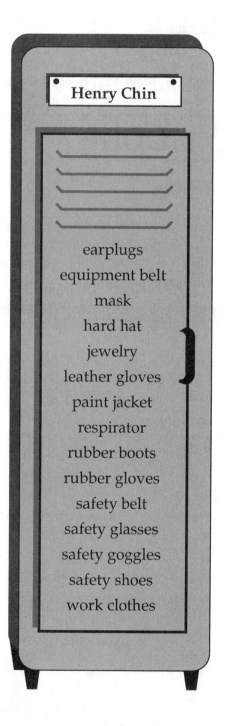
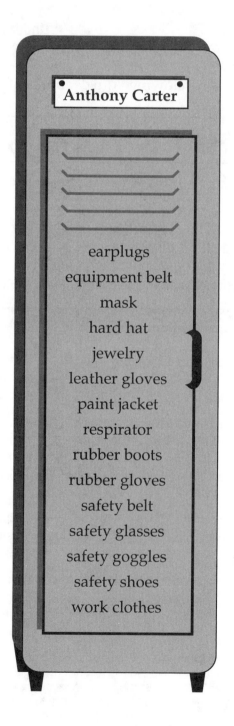

Henry Chin

earplugs
equipment belt
mask
hard hat
jewelry
leather gloves
paint jacket
respirator
rubber boots
rubber gloves
safety belt
safety glasses
safety goggles
safety shoes
work clothes

Anthony Carter

earplugs
equipment belt
mask
hard hat
jewelry
leather gloves
paint jacket
respirator
rubber boots
rubber gloves
safety belt
safety glasses
safety goggles
safety shoes
work clothes

Using Graphs
(reading and interpreting bar graphs)

Look at the three bar graphs that follow. Read the titles. Then answer the questions.

1. What is the title of the first graph? _____

2. What is the title of the second graph? _____

3. What is the title of the third graph? _____

4. Are all of the graphs from the same year? _____

5. Are all of the graphs from the same company? _____

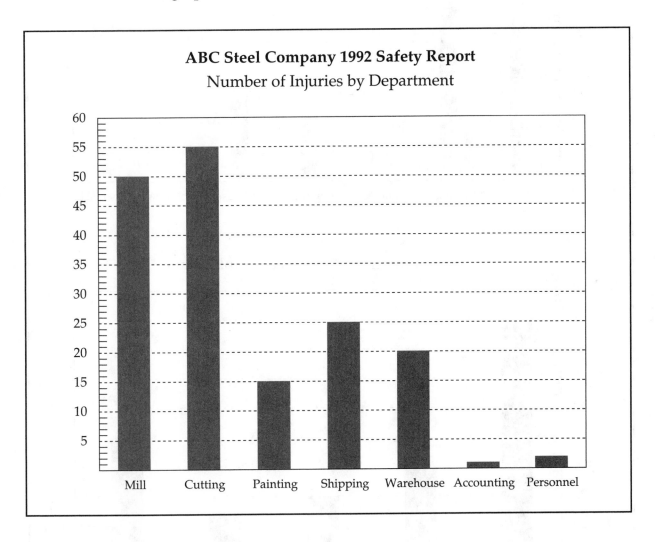

ABC Steel Company 1992 Safety Report

Number of Injuries by Department

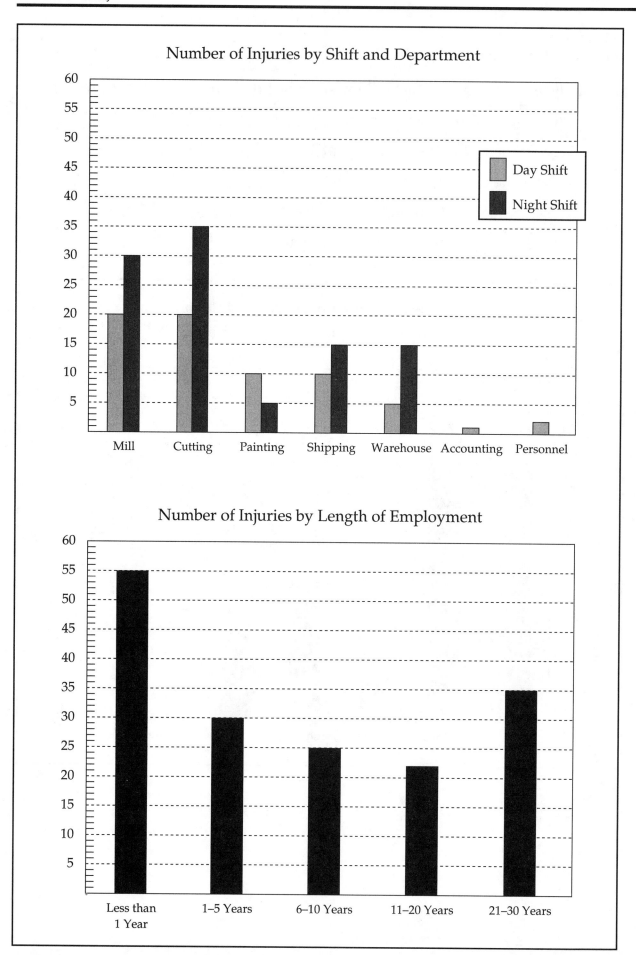

Number of Injuries by Shift and Department

Number of Injuries by Length of Employment

Study the first graph. Then answer the questions.

6.   How many injuries did the shipping department have? _____

7.   How many injuries did the mill have? _____

8.   Which department has more injuries—painting or warehouse?

_____

9.   Which departments have the most injuries?_____

10.   Which departments have the fewest injuries? _____

11.   Why do you think that the departments in question #9 have the most

injuries?_____

12.   Why do you think that the departments in question #10 have the fewest

injuries?_____

Study the second graph. Then answer the questions.

13.   Which departments don't have a night shift?_____

14.   Which shift has more injuries—the day shift or the night shift? _____

15.   a. How many workers were injured in the cutting department on the day

shift? _____

b. How many workers were injured in the cutting department on the night

shift? _____

c. What is the total? _____

d. Look at the first graph. How many workers were injured in the cutting

department?_____

Study the third graph. Then answer the questions.

16. Which group of employees has the most injuries? _____

17. Which group of employees has the fewest injuries? _____

18. Which group of workers has fewer injuries—the employees who have

worked 1–5 years or 6–10 years? _____

19. Why do you think that workers with little experience (less than one year)

have a lot of injuries? _____

20. Why do you think that workers with a lot of experience (21–30 years) have

many injuries? _____

UNIT 4 *Interacting with Co-workers*

Before You Read
(making predictions, relating experiences to reading, establishing prior knowledge)

Credit: Florida News Bureau

Credit: U.S. Air Force photo

Credit: Courtesy of Tupperware Home Parties

Talk about these photographs with a partner.

Write your answers on the lines.

1. Where are these people? _____

   _____

2. What are they doing? _____

   _____

3. Why are these photographs in a book about work? _____

   _____

4. Are there any social activities where you work? _____

   Which ones? _____

   _____

Reading About Work

Bowling Buddies

Jack, Bob, and Loi are having lunch in the company cafeteria. Luis is walking with his tray, looking for a place to sit.

JACK: Hey, Luis! Over here! How's it going?

LUIS: (puts his tray down) Okay. I'm going to get some ketchup for my hot dog. Just a minute. (Luis sits down.) Hi, everybody!

JACK: Listen, Luis. The other guys and I were talking about forming a bowling team. Do you want to join?

LUIS: Well, I don't know. I don't know how to bowl.

JACK: That's okay. We'll show you. It's really easy to learn.

LUIS: When are you are going to bowl? Right after work?

BOB: No. We'll go home and eat supper first. We'll meet at the Bowl-A-Rama Alley at 7:30. How does that sound?

LUIS: I don't know, fellas. I'm taking an English class at night.

JACK: Which night?

LUIS: Actually, it's two nights—Tuesdays and Thursdays.

BOB: Well, this will work out fine—bowling is on Wednesdays.

LUIS: Gee, fellas. It's nice of you to ask, but—

JACK: Come on, Luis. It will be a good way to get to know some of the guys better.

LOI: Yeah, I joined the bowling team last year, Luis. We had a lot of fun, and it's good exercise, too! After bowling, we always went out for a pizza. I practiced my English, and I learned a lot!

BOB: Yeah, and in the spring, after bowling is over, we'll start our softball games.

LUIS: One thing at a time! Okay, guys, I'll take you up on your offer. Thanks for asking me to join. Now—I never figured this out—can you tell me how to put all five fingers in those three holes?

CRANKSHAFT

CRANKSHAFT © Mediagraphics, Inc. Reprinted with permission of UNIVERSAL PRESS SYNDICATE. All rights reserved.

Understanding New Words

(expanding vocabulary, understanding new words through context)

Read these sentences with a partner. Decide together if *a* or *b* describes the underlined words. Circle *a* or *b*.

1. Jack asks Luis, "<u>How's it going</u>?"

   a. Where are you going?

   b. How are you?

2. Later, Jack asks Luis, "Do you want to <u>join</u> our bowling team?"

   a. be a member of

   b. come to the bowling alley and watch

3. Bob says, "We'll meet at the Bowl-A-Rama Alley at 7:30. <u>How does that sound</u>?"

   a. Is that okay with you?

   b. Did you hear me?

4. Luis says, "<u>Actually</u>, my class is two nights a week."

   a. Now

   b. Really

5. Bob says that everything will <u>work out fine</u> because bowling is on Wednesdays and Luis's class is on Tuesdays and Thursdays.

   a. be good exercise

   b. have a good result

6. In the spring, when bowling <u>is over</u>, the men will start to play softball.

   a. is finished

   b. starts

7. Luis says, "Okay, guys, I'll <u>take you up on</u> your offer.

   a. think about

   b. accept

8. Luis never <u>figured out</u> how to put all five fingers in the three holes of the bowling ball.

   a. understood

   b. thought about

Understanding the Reading

(checking literal comprehension)

Matching: Work with a partner. Find the words in Part A and Part B that make sentences. Then write the sentences on the lines.

Part A	Part B
1. At first, Luis doesn't want to join	form softball teams.
2. The men are going to bowl at	to get to know the other workers.
3. Luis is studying English two	✔ the bowling team.
4. Loi says that bowling is good	nights a week.
5. Jack says that bowling is a good way	exercise and a lot of fun.
6. In the spring, after bowling is over, the men will	accept Jack's offer to join the team.
7. Finally, Luis decides to	to fit his fingers in the holes of the bowling ball.
8. Luis doesn't understand how	7:30 on Wednesdays.

1. At first, Luis doesn't want to join the bowling team.

2. _____

3. _____

4. _____

5. _____

6. _____

7. _____

8. _____

Discussing

Activity 1: Two-by-two conversation *(listening for specific information)*

Here is a conversation between two co-workers, Rita and Betty. On this page is Rita's side of the conversation. On the next page is Betty's side of the conversation. Work with a partner. Rita begins the conversation.

Start with Number 1. Read *1A* or *1B* to your partner. Your partner will listen and respond with number *1A* or *1B* on the next page. Listen carefully to what your partner says, and respond by choosing number *2A* or *2B*, and so on.

Rita

1
A: Hi, Betty! How are you? You weren't at work last week.
B: Hi, Betty? Where were you? You weren't at work last week.

2
A: How nice! Disneyland is one of my favorite places. Say, did you hear about the company picnic?
B: I'm sorry that you were sick, but I'm glad that you're feeling better now. By the way, did you know that Barbara is going to retire next week?

3
A: Yes, we're going to have a party for her at the office next Friday—her last day.
B: On Saturday from 11:00–3:00 in the park across the street. You know—where the grills are.

4
A: Sure. It's going to be potluck style. I have a sign-up sheet at my desk. We still need desserts, salads, and meat dishes.
B: Yes. You don't have to bring anything to the picnic, but the admission is $2.00 per person. It's going to be better than last year. We're going to have a clown and pony rides for the children.

5
A: No problem. You can even pay on Saturday at the picnic if you want to.
B: Fine. See you then. Oh, I almost forgot—we're collecting money to buy Barbara a gift.

Here is Betty's side of the conversation. Rita begins the conversation. Listen carefully to her before you answer. Respond with *1A* or *1B* on this (Betty's) page. Then wait for Rita to answer you. Next choose number *2A* or *2B* and so on.

Betty

1
- A: Well, I'm fine now. I was sick for about a week.
- B: I was on vacation. I went with some friends to Disneyland in California.

2
- A: She is? No, I didn't know that! Are we going to do something special?
- B: No, I didn't, but I'm glad that you told me. My family always enjoys the picnic. When is it?

3
- A: Can I bring something to the party?
- B: Are we going to cook hot dogs and hamburgers on the grills like last year?

4
- A: Okay. I'll think about what I want to bring. I'll talk to you at break about it.
- B: That's a lot for only $2.00! I'll pay you at lunch, okay?

5
- A: Okay. I'll sign up for the food and give you the money at break. Bye.
- B: No, I'll give you the money at lunch. See you then.

Activity 2 *(using creative thinking to complete a conversation)*

Complete the following conversation. Practice it with a partner.

ART: Hi, Jack! How are you? I didn't see you at work the past two weeks. Where were you?

JACK: _____

ART: Well, since you were on vacation for about two weeks, did you know that Bill Thompson is retiring?

JACK: _____

ART: We're going to have a farewell dinner next Thursday at a restaurant.

JACK: _____

ART: It's going to be at 6:00 at John's Steakhouse.

JACK: _____

ART: I'm collecting the money for the dinner and for a gift, too.

JACK: _____

ART: It's $10.00 for the dinner, and we're asking $5.00 from each person for the gift.

JACK: _____

ART: Great! I'll see you there!

Activity 3 *(relating the reading to work experiences)*

Discuss these questions in class.
1. What social activities are there where you work?
2. How do you find out about the activities?
3. Which activities do you participate in?

Writing
(making a poster or flyer)

Read the flyer below for an ice skating party for Excel Corporation employees. Then make a poster or a flyer for a company social activity such as a picnic, a Christmas party, a volleyball game, or an activity that you know about at your company.

Include the name of the activity and some information about it, the date, the place, and the time. Remember to invite everybody!

Reading at Work

(scanning to locate specific information)

Learning about Different Reasons for Reading

Sometimes we read for information, and sometimes we read for fun. When we read for fun, we may read quickly and only the parts that interest us.

On page 49 are some excerpts from the company newsletter from Doyle's Department Store. Read the following articles *quickly* to find the main ideas and then answer the questions.

Understanding the Reading

1. Which paragraph(s) talk about weddings? _____6_____

2. About birthdays? _____

3. About new babies? _____

4. About education? _____

5. About vacations? _____

6. About deaths? _____

7. About a picnic? _____

8. About exercise? _____

9. About new employees? _____

10. About retirement? _____

11. About a diet class? _____

Discussing Doyle's Departments

IN GENERAL . . .

1 Doyle's annual picnic will be held on Saturday, Sept. 22, in the Thatcher Woods, located at Belmont St. and 1st Avenue. All employees should contact their picnic representatives for details.

2 JCK Fitness Center gives you the tools necessary to TRY HARDER. The fitness center has pressure resistant and Universal equipment, stationary bicycles, Stairmaster, running machine, floor mat, aerobics classes, and nutrition/fitness classes. The instructors are knowledgeable and persistent in helping you achieve your personal goals.

3 Starting in September there will be a diet exchange class. This class was designed to provide nutritional awareness. To become a member in the class you must sign-up at the fitness center. Classes will be held there during the daytime hours of 11 a.m. to approximately 1:30 p.m. Classes will last about 45 minutes to an hour. Check with the fitness center personnel for the exact days and times.

4 Unfortunately, we would like to extend our condolences to the following employees on the loss of loved ones: Jackie Ashe and Miguel Gomez.

ACCOUNTING

5 Speaking of educational achievements, Louise Mason of Data Processing recently received a bachelor of arts degree in management from National Education University. Take a bow, Louise.

6 Congratulations to Mary E. Smith on her marriage to Thomas J. Anderson. They were married on June 7, and will be making their home in Pleasantown. The Accounting Department celebrated with a lovely bridal shower given in her honor thanks to the effort of Marge Booth. Our best wishes to the newlyweds.

FIRST FLOOR

7 Welcome aboard to Letty Rodriguez, Brenda Jackson, and Vito Scati, who are new to the 1st floor depts.

8 News flash! Fred McKee, manager of Housewares, has announced his retirement as of Sept. 30. You will be missed, Fred.

9 The new manager of Electronics, José Garcia and his wife recently had a new baby girl. Ileana was born on Aug. 4, and came home on José's birthday, Aug. 6. Mom and baby are doing fine. Congratulations, José, on your new arrival. We hope you will not have too many sleepless nights!

SECOND FLOOR

10 Congratulations to some new parents on the 2nd floor. Klaus Schmidt has welcomed another girl to his family. Renata Bloom is a new mother of a little girl.

11 Welcome back to Sally White, who was on sick leave. We're glad you're back! Mabel Johnson traveled to Louisiana recently to her first high school class reunion. She enjoyed seeing classmates she has not seen since they were 18 years old. The class reunion was held for everyone who had attended Central High between the years 1935 to 1969. There were approximately 650 people from across the country who returned for this reunion. Almost everyone had changed so much they were only recognizable by their name tags. Plans are being made for the next class reunion.

SHIPPING AND RECEIVING

12 Welcome back to Joan Ross, who is returning from a two-week trip to Hawaii. Welcome back to Delbert Price from his trip to Disneyland and Georgia. Welcome back to Al Ruiz who had just returned from vacation. Sam Cooper will be going to Florida for a two week vacation. George Wilson will be going to Wisconsin to catch the big one that got away. Hua Nguyen will be going to New Jersey and then to Canada. Sylvia Cantu is preparing to attend a family reunion.

13 Belated happy birthday to Connie Short and Alicia Ramirez.

Listening
(listening for specific information; problem solving)

Rosa and Mattie are planning a baby shower and going-away party for Kathy, who is going to leave her job very soon. Listen to the tape. Decide what each person is going to bring to the party. Put a check (✔) by that person's name. Also decide how much Rosa and Mattie can spend on the wrapping paper and card for Kathy.

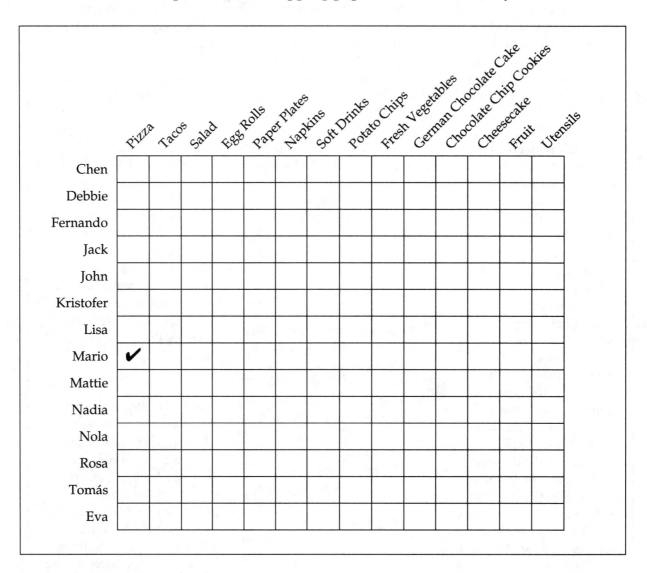

	Pizza	Tacos	Salad	Egg Rolls	Paper Plates	Napkins	Soft Drinks	Potato Chips	Fresh Vegetables	German Chocolate Cake	Chocolate Chip Cookies	Cheesecake	Fruit	Utensils
Chen														
Debbie														
Fernando														
Jack														
John														
Kristofer														
Lisa														
Mario	✔													
Mattie														
Nadia														
Nola														
Rosa														
Tomás														
Eva														

Work in small groups. After listening to the tape, insert the correct numbers on the lines below.

1. Number of people attending party _____

2. Each person will contribute $_____

3. The caterer will cost $_____

4. The present will cost $_____

5. Money for wrapping paper and card $_____

Using Math

(adding 3-digit numbers in columns)

When people bowl, they receive one point for each pin that they knock down. Look at the bowling record below.

To figure out which team won each game:

a.   Add the columns going down (↓) (1st Game, 2nd Game, 3rd Game). ①

b.   Compare the results of the two teams. Which team has more points (knocked down more pins)? Put an *X* in the circles next to *Game Won by.* ②

To find out which team knocked down the most pins for all three games:

c.   Add the totals for each person for each game going across (→). ③

d.   Then add the totals for each player going down. ④ This number is the same as the subtotals for each game going across. ⑤

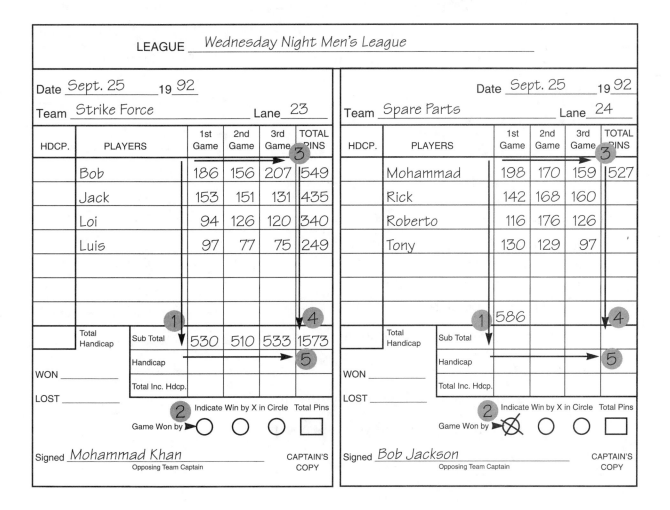

UNIT 5   *Interacting with Supervisors*

Before You Read
(making predictions, relating experiences to reading, establishing prior knowledge)

Cathy

Talk about this comic strip with a partner.

Write your answers on the lines.

1. Who is Mr. Pinkley? _____

2. Why are his employees complaining? _____

    _____

3. What do you think they want Mr. Pinkley to do? _____

    _____

4. Do you communicate problems to your boss? _____

    How do you communicate problems to him or her? _____

    _____

5. Do you talk about other things with your supervisor? _____

    If you do, what other things do you talk about? _____

    _____

Reading About Work

Anna's Problems

Mr. Jones, the supervisor at Favorite Toys Company, is talking to his workers about production problems.

MR. JONES: I looked at our production for the past month, and I compared it with the production levels of two and three months ago. We have a big problem here. Our production is down by almost 10%. You know that we are making the most popular toy for little girls—the Allison Doll. The Christmas season is coming, and we can't fill our orders fast enough. We need to increase our production by 15%. I'm counting on you! If we don't meet our goal, I will have to let some of you go. Okay, back to work! Oh, Anna—can I see you for a minute?

ANNA: Of course, Mr. Jones.

MR. JONES: Anna, I'm worried about your work performance.

ANNA: Why, Mr. Jones?

MR. JONES: In the past, you were one of my best workers, but the quality of your work and your attendance are not so good anymore. A couple of times it was difficult to replace you on the crew. I don't want to let you go, but if your work doesn't improve . . . . And Anna, please look at me when I talk to you. When you look at the floor, I think that you aren't listening to me. Now, I need to know—what is the problem? Why are you absent so much and what happened to the quality of your work?

ANNA: Well, nothing . . . really nothing. I'll try harder. I promise.

MR. JONES: Well, I'm giving you a verbal warning. If your work and attendance don't improve, I'll put you on probation. And you know that the next step is to let you go.

ANNA: Yes, Mr. Jones.

(Later, Anna is talking to her best friend at work, Cecilia.)

ANNA: Mr. Jones talked to me after the meeting. He's not happy with my work.

CECILIA: Well, I think that you need to tell Mr. Jones about your family problems. It's hard for you to give all of your attention to your job. Your daughter is in the hospital and your father recently died.

ANNA: I know—I'm always thinking about those things. Cecilia, I don't want to lose my job.

CECILIA: Why don't you talk to Mr. Jones? He'll understand your situation.

ANNA: Oh, I don't want to talk to him about my personal problems. That's not right. I can only talk about work problems with my supervisor.

CECILIA: But Anna, if your personal problems affect your work, then they *are* work problems.

ANNA: Well, I'll think about it. Thanks for talking to me about this, Cecilia. I have to do something because I can't lose my job. I don't need any more problems.

Understanding New Words

(expanding vocabulary, understanding new words through context)

Read these pairs of sentences with a partner. Decide if the meaning of the sentences is the same or different. Circle *same* or *different*.

1. Mr. Jones counts on his employees to do a good job.   *same*   *different*
    Mr. Jones depends on his employees to do a good job.

2. I'm worried about your work performance.   *same*   *different*
    I'm worried about how you do your job.

3. Mr. Jones' goal is to increase production by 15%.   *same*   *different*
    Mr. Jones wants to increase production by 15%.

4. Mr. Jones says that he may let Anna go.   *same*   *different*
    Mr. Jones says that he may give Anna a promotion.

5. A couple of times it was difficult to replace Anna   *same*   *different*
    on the crew.
    A couple of times it was difficult to find another
    person to work for Anna.

6. Mr. Jones is giving Anna a verbal warning.   *same*   *different*
    Mr. Jones is giving Anna a piece of paper that says
    something bad may happen to her.

7. Anna's personal problems affect her work.   *same*   *different*
    Anna's personal problems make the quality of
    her work go down.

Understanding the Reading

(identifying specific details, checking literal comprehension)

Read the following story about the problems at Favorite Toys Company. There are 14 mistakes in the story. Work with a partner and correct the mistakes. Two examples are done for you.

Mr. Jones is talking to his workers. He tells them that production is ~~up~~ *down* this month. The factory makes the most popular toy for little boys. Mr. Jones wants to increase production by 10% for the Halloween season. If the employees *don't* meet their goal, Mr. Jones will have to let some of them go.

Mr. Jones wants to speak to Cecilia because he is happy with her work. Her attendance is very good. It was easy for him to replace Anna on the crew. Mr. Jones thinks that Anna is listening to him when she doesn't look at him. He wants Anna to tell him what the problem is. Mr. Jones gives Anna a written warning. He says that the next step is to let her go.

Cecilia thinks that Anna needs to tell Mr. Jones about her problems. Anna's husband is in the hospital and her mother recently died. Cecilia thinks that Mr. Jones will understand why Anna can't concentrate on her work.

Discussing

Activity 1: Role play *(using critical thinking, empathizing with a character)*

Below are four *role plays*. In a role play, students take different parts and act them out. In these role plays, Student *A* is the employee, and Student *B* is the supervisor. They will "act out" their parts.

1. An employee at Doyle's (Student A) does not always treat the customers well. The employee also chews gum and makes mistakes on the cash register. The supervisor (Student B) gave a verbal warning to the employee. The supervisor now feels that it is necessary to take some stronger action against the employee.

2. An employee at the Sweet Tooth Bakery (Student A) is having some personal problems (financial and marital). Student A is often absent, comes to work late, and does not concentrate on his or her work. Until recently, the employee was an excellent worker and the supervisor (Student B) wanted to give him or her a promotion. The supervisor really wants to help the employee. The employee doesn't want to talk about his or her problems with the supervisor because in the employee's culture, it is not appropriate to discuss personal problems at work.

3. Student A is a new employee in the shipping department at the ABC Steel Company. The supervisor (Student B) in the shipping department is very friendly. He or she always asks the employees about their families, and likes to arrange picnics, volleyball games, and softball games with the employees. The supervisor asks the new employee to join the company softball team. The new employee feels very uncomfortable around supervisors and doesn't want to spend time socially with the boss. The supervisor wants the new employee to join the team in order to have fun and to get to know the other employees better. The supervisor feels this is good for the company and good for the new employee.

4. Student A is an employee at XYZ Steel Company. The employee feels that the boss (Student B) ignores him or her. The boss always talks to the other employees, offers them overtime, and gives some of them promotions, but doesn't pay attention to Student A. Student A feels that he or she does a good job: is always on time, meets goals on the production line, and gets along well with co-workers. The employee wants to talk to the boss to find out what the problem is. The boss doesn't like the employee very much because another employee told the boss some things about Student A that aren't true, but the boss believes them.

Activity 2 *(relating the reading to work situations)*

Discuss these questions in class.

1. What are some of the ways that you can communicate with your supervisor?
2. What kinds of things do you discuss with your supervisor?
3. Why is it important to have good communication with your supervisor?

Reading at Work

Understanding New Words

(expanding vocabulary, understanding new words through context)

Read the sentences below. Find and circle the underlined words in the reading.

1. The underline watched and listened to the actors on stage.
2. Elsa was sure that she could do the job. She felt confident.
3. What is your point of view about the new company policy on absences? In my opinion, it is better than the old policy because it permits us two extra sick days each year.
4. The company plans to maintain or keep its current level of production.
5. You don't have to worry about retaliation at ABC Steel Company. You can say what you think and nothing bad will happen to you because you expressed your point of view.

Understanding the Reading

(checking literal comprehension)

In Unit 4, you read a page from Doyle's company newsletter. It contained personal information about the employees at Doyle's. Sometimes companies include articles of special interest in their newsletters. Following is an article about the importance of communication between workers and management at Doyle's. Read the article and discuss the questions with your class.

The Open Door of Communication

A Doyle's employee with an idea or a complaint always has an audience, according to Human Resources Personnel.

"We want people to feel confident in expressing opinions to co-workers and managers," said Ivana Novak, Vice President of Human Resources.

Doyle's open communication policy means that every point of view is important.

"People's ideas helped to build this company," Ms. Novak said. "Your point of view, even if it's different from everyone else's, could be the one that the company decides is best."

The goal of Doyle's open communication policy is to make every employee feel like he or she is a valuable part of the company.

Doyle's maintains open communication through formal store meetings and informal meetings, daily conversations and employee suggestion boxes.

"If employees have problems, they should feel free to talk with their supervisor or anyone in management without fear of retaliation," Ms. Novak said. "If there is a problem, we want to take care of it right away."

"Open communication creates a good working environment. This positively affects customer service, and that's good for business," Ms. Novak said.

"People coming into the company are often surprised by our open communications policy," she said. "I hope we can continue to listen to our employees' concerns and work to solve their problems."

If an employee feels his or her supervisor isn't listening, Ms. Novak tells that employee to see someone at a higher level or in Human Resources.

"We'll do what we can to resolve any communication problem," she said.

1. What is Doyle's open communication policy?
2. What is the goal of Doyle's open communication policy?
3. How does Doyle's maintain open communication?
4. If employees have problems, who can they talk to?
5. What are the benefits of the open communication policy at Doyle's?

Listening

(listening for specific information, sequencing information)

Mr. Coates is the shipping and receiving supervisor at Doyle's. He is standing on the receiving dock and talking to one of his employees, Joe. Joe unloaded 12 boxes of merchandise. Mr. Coates is reading the inventory numbers on the boxes to Joe. Joe is checking the numbers off on his inventory list. Listen to the tape. When Mr. Coates calls out a number to Joe, look at the inventory list, and put a check (✔) next to that number on the list.

Inventory number (✔)		Order	Inventory Number (✔)		Order
A 60 F 09	✔		C 90 D 41		
E 16 F 09			Z 90 T 41		
B 40 C 82			Y 35 C 19		
V 14 C 82			I 35 Z 19		
I 60 S 09			Y 18 A 37		
E 60 F 09			I 80 H 37		
K 27 I 55			V 30 S 57		
Q 27 I 55			B 13 Z 57		
N 03 A 78			Q 50 A 73		
M 03 H 78			Q 15 H 73		

After checking off the numbers of the boxes, Mr. Coates wants Joe to stack the boxes in a certain order. He wants Joe to make two stacks. Then Joe can put the boxes on a cart and deliver them to the appropriate departments in the store. Listen to the order that Mr. Coates wants. In the column marked *Order,* write number *1* next to the inventory number *1* that you hear first, number *2* next to the inventory number that you hear second, and so on.

Using Math

(reading and understanding an earnings statement, adding, subtracting, and multiplying decimals)

The Excel Company is changing its payroll system. The company is going to issue its paychecks every *two* weeks (biweekly) instead of *every* week. Look at the earnings statement below and answer the questions.

EARNINGS STATEMENT

EMPLOYEE NAME					SOCIAL SECURITY NO.		REG
RUIZ, ANTONIO					352 44 1689		——

OFF	P/P END DATE	PAY PLAN	GR	SALARY	STATE CODE & EXEMPS/DEPDNTS	FED TAX & EXEMPS	HEALTH CODE	FEGLI	FISCAL DIST CODE
—	11 15 92	—	—	——	IL 001	1 00	——		——

EARNINGS THIS STATEMENT	HOURS	AMOUNT		DEDUCTIONS THIS STATEMENT	
REGULAR	80.00	560.00		FED. TAX	40.00
OVERTIME				STATE TAX	11.71
HOL. WORKED				HEALTH INS.	14.32
NIGHT DIFF.				FICA	39.20
SUN				LIFE INS.	8.09
				PENSION	15.75
				CHARITY	
				UNION DUES	5.00
GROSS		560.00			
TOTAL DEDUCTIONS		134.07			
NET PAY		425.93			

1. Who is this earnings statement for? _____

2. When does the pay period end? _____

3. Did Antonio work overtime? _____

4. How much did Antonio pay in federal income tax? $_____

5. When Antonio's paycheck was weekly, how much were his union dues?
    (*Hint:* Half of $5.00 =) $_____

6. How much does Antonio earn per hour? (*Hint:* 560 ÷ 80 =) $_____

7. Antonio earned $560.00 (gross earnings). Does he have $560.00 to spend?
    _____ Why not? _____

8. How much of his earnings can he spend (take-home pay)? $_____
    What is another name for this pay? _____

Math Help

A. To answer the questions below, you will need to know how to add, subtract, and multiply decimals. Decimals are parts of whole numbers. When we talk about money, we use decimals. For example, $13.00 consists of a whole number, 13. A price such as $13.42 consists of a whole number, 13, and a decimal .42 (42 cents is part of $1, which is a whole number).

B. Adding decimals is the same as adding whole numbers. Remember to line up the decimal points.

EXAMPLES:
$$\begin{array}{r} \$4.13 \\ 1.29 \\ +\,.77 \\ \hline \$6.19 \\ \uparrow \end{array} \qquad \begin{array}{r} \$12.46 \\ 9.33 \\ +\,1.05 \\ \hline \$22.84 \\ \uparrow \end{array}$$

C. Subtracting decimals is the same as subtracting whole numbers. Remember to line up the decimal points.

EXAMPLES:
$$\begin{array}{r} \$15.98 \\ -10.71 \\ \hline \$\ 5.27 \\ \uparrow \end{array} \qquad \begin{array}{r} \$43.57 \\ -21.08 \\ \hline \$22.49 \\ \uparrow \end{array}$$

D. Multiplying decimals is *almost* the same as multiplying whole numbers. Only one thing is different—you have to decide where to put the decimal point.

First multiply the problem as you normally do.

$$\begin{array}{r} \$4.25 \quad \text{(minimum wage)} \\ \times \quad 8 \quad \text{(hours worked)} \\ \hline \$3400 \end{array}$$

Now you need to insert the decimal point in the answer. Count the number of decimal places in both numbers.

$$\begin{array}{r} \$4.25 \quad \text{2 decimal places} \\ \times \quad 8 \quad \text{+0 decimal places} \\ \hline \text{2 decimal places} \end{array}$$

To decide where to put the decimal point, count the same number of decimal places (2) in the answer to the problem. Count from right to left. Put the decimal point next to the last number that you counted.

$$\begin{array}{r} \$4.25 \\ \times \quad 8 \\ \hline \$34.00 \end{array}$$

The following is Antonio's earnings statement for the next pay period in November, which includes the holiday, Thanksgiving. Antonio worked that day. He received double-time (two times his hourly wage). He also worked one Sunday and received time-and-a-half (his hourly wage plus one half of his hourly wage). Answer the following questions about Antonio's earnings.

EARNINGS STATEMENT

EMPLOYEE NAME					SOCIAL SECURITY NO.		REG
RUIZ, ANTONIO					352 44 1689		—

OFF	P/P END DATE	PAY PLAN	GR	SALARY	STATE CODE & EXEMPS/DEPDNTS	FED TAX & EXEMPS	HEALTH CODE	FEGLI	FISCAL DIST CODE
—	11 30 92	—	—	—	IL 001	1 00	—	—	—

EARNINGS THIS STATEMENT	HOURS	AMOUNT		DEDUCTIONS THIS STATEMENT	
REGULAR	72 00			FED. TAX	40 00
OVERTIME				STATE TAX	11 71
HOL. WORKED	8 00			HEALTH INS.	14 32
NIGHT DIFF.				FICA	49 00
SUN	8 00			LIFE INS.	8 09
				PENSION	15 75
				CHARITY	
				UNION DUES	5 00
GROSS					
TOTAL DEDUCTIONS					
NET PAY					

1. How much does Antonio earn per hour when he works a holiday and he gets double-time? (*Hint:* $7.00 \times 2 =$) $_____

2. How much does Antonio earn on a holiday? (*Hint:* Answer from #1 x 8 hours) $_____

3. How much does Antonio earn per hour on a Sunday? (*Hint:* Half of 7 is 3.5, so time-and-a-half is   7.00   (hourly earnings)

    +3.50   (half of hourly earnings)
    ———
    $_____

4. How much does Antonio earn on a Sunday? (*Hint:* Answer from #3 x 8 hours =) $_____

5. How much did Antonio earn (gross pay) for the second pay period in November? $_____ (Calculate below.)

    a. REGULAR TIME

        72 hours $7.00

        (9 days)   x   72

            $_____

    d. Add your answers together

        REGULAR TIME $_____

        HOL. WORKED $_____

        SUN. $_____

        TOTAL $_____

    b. HOL. WORKED

        8 hours $14.00

        (1 day)   x   8

            $_____

    c. SUN.

        8 hours $10.50

        (1 day)   x   8

            $_____

6. Now, fill in the numbers on Antonio's earnings statement (his deductions are filled in for you.) Figure out his gross earnings and his net earnings. (*Hint:* Add *DEDUCTIONS*, then subtract *TOTAL DEDUCTIONS* from *GROSS.*)

Writing

(writing a suggestion for improving a work situation)

Sometimes employees have ideas that they would like to tell the supervisor, but they don't feel comfortable talking directly with the boss. One way that an employee can communicate is through the *suggestion box*. An employee may have an idea to save the company some money, a way to increase production, or an idea to make the workplace safer. The employee can *write* the idea on a piece of paper and put it in the suggestion box. Sometimes there are prizes for the best suggestion.

EXAMPLE: Wing Su, who works at Diamond's Food Store, put this idea in the suggestion box to help save the store some money.

I have a suggestion for the problem of spoiled fruit and vegetables in
our produce section. Now, we throw them away. I suggest taking the
fruit and vegetables when they are very ripe (but not spoiled) and
putting them on a reduced-price rack. If people buy this produce,
Diamond's will not lose money.
Thank you,
Wing Su

Think of a way that you can increase production, save your company some money, or make your workplace safer or better. Write your suggestion below.

_____

_____

_____

_____

_____

_____

_____

_____

_____

_____

_____

UNIT 6 *Personalities and Conflicts*

Before You Read

(making predictions, relating experiences to reading, establishing prior knowledge)

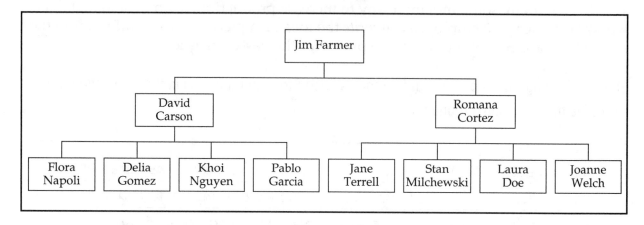

Talk about this diagram with a partner.

Write your answers on the lines.

1. How many supervisors are there in this diagram? _____

2. Who is Laura's supervisor? _____

3. If Laura has a problem with a co-worker, who can she talk to?_____

   _____

4. If Laura has a problem with her supervisor, who should she talk to? _____

   _____

5. What do you do when you have a problem with a co-worker?_____

   _____

6. What do you do when you have a problem with your supervisor? _____

   _____

Reading About Work

Who Do You Talk To?

Sammy and Tom work in food service at Eastlake Hospital. Their job is to put food trays on carts and take the trays to the patients. Later, they take the trays back to the kitchen. They wash dishes and clean the kitchen until they deliver more meals. They deliver lunch between 11:00 A.M. and 12:30 P.M., and they deliver dinner between 4:00 P.M. and 5:30 P.M. Sammy and Tom need to follow a tight schedule to finish all of their duties.

Tom and Sammy are having a problem with the kitchen crew. There are some new workers, and they are still learning their jobs. They don't get the food ready on time for Tom and Sammy. Tom wants to discuss the problem with Mrs. Sims, the manager of food service.

(Tom and Sammy are talking to each other.)

TOM: You know, Sammy, we need to do something! The kitchen crew doesn't get the food ready on time, and we get behind schedule. We're responsible for finishing all of our duties before quitting time. We need to talk to Mrs. Sims about the problem in the kitchen.

SAMMY: I know, Tom, but I don't like to complain. Maybe if we work faster—

TOM: No. We're doing our job correctly. The problem is in the kitchen. We need to talk to Mrs. Sims.

SAMMY: No, I don't think that's a good idea.

TOM: Why not?

SAMMY: Oh, I don't know. Maybe we can talk to Mr. Ortiz.

TOM: But he's not our supervisor. We should discuss problems with our immediate supervisor. It's important to follow the hospital's rules for reporting problems.

SAMMY: I would feel more comfortable talking to Mr. Ortiz.

TOM: Why? Mrs. Sims is very nice and she is always very helpful.

SAMMY: Well . . . I don't think that you will understand.

TOM: Sammy, you and I don't always see eye to eye, but we usually talk about our differences.

SAMMY: Well, in my country, women don't work. So, there are no women supervisors. I never had a woman supervisor before. It's hard for me to talk to Mrs. Sims about a work problem.

TOM: You know, a few years ago, we didn't have any women supervisors here, either. But everything changes! Eastlake is a great place to work. My supervisors always try to help me to do a good job. And Mrs. Sims is one of the best. Come on—we'll go to her office together. I'll talk this time.

SAMMY: Thanks for your help, Tom! It's not easy to live in a new country, but you make it a little easier!

Understanding New Words and Phrases
(expanding vocabulary, understanding new words through context)

Read the following pairs of sentences with a partner. Decide together if the meaning of the sentences is the same or different. Circle *same* or *different*.

1. There are many patients at Eastlake Hospital.   *same*   *different*
   There are many sick people at Eastlake Hospital.

2. Sammy and Tom deliver food to the patients.   *same*   *different*
   Sammy and Tom take food to the patients.

3. Sammy and Tom have a tight schedule to follow.   *same*   *different*
   Sammy and Tom can take as much time as they
   want to finish their duties.

4. Tom and Sammy get behind schedule.   *same*   *different*
   Tom and Sammy finish their work early.

5. Sammy doesn't want to complain to Mrs. Sims.   *same*   *different*
   Sammy doesn't want to tell Mrs. Sims that
   he is unhappy.

6. Tom and Sammy need to talk to Mrs. Sims   *same*   *different*
   because she is their immediate supervisor.
   Tom and Sammy need to talk to Mrs. Sims
   because she is their boss.

7. Sammy and Tom don't always see eye to eye.   *same*   *different*
   Sammy and Tom don't always agree completely.

Understanding the Reading

(identifying details, checking literal comprehension)

A. TRUE/FALSE: Read these sentences with a partner. Decide together if they are *true* or *false*. Circle *T* for true and *F* for false.

1. Sammy and Tom work in a restaurant.   T   (F)

2. They deliver breakfast to the patients.   T   F

3. The new workers in the kitchen don't know their jobs very well.   T   F

4. Tom wants to talk to Mrs. Sims about the problem in the kitchen.   T   F

5. In Sammy's country, there are many women supervisors.   T   F

6. Mr. Ortiz is Sammy's immediate supervisor.   T   F

7. When there's a problem at the hospital, there are rules for the employees to follow.   T   F

8. It's easy for Sammy to discuss work problems with a woman supervisor.   T   F

9. Tom likes his supervisors.   T   F

10. Finally, Sammy decides to go with Tom to talk to Mrs. Sims.   T   F

B. There are five *false* sentences in Exercise A. Rewrite the false sentences to make them true.

1. Sammy and Tom work in a hospital.

2. _____

3. _____

4. _____

5. _____

Discussing

Activity 1: Role plays *(evaluating reasons for actions, empathizing with a character)*

1. Student A is a supervisor. He or she feels that employees should receive recognition for doing a good job. Each month, the supervisor chooses an "Employee of the Month." The supervisor puts up the employee's photograph for everyone to see. Student B is from a country where public recognition is embarrassing. This month, the supervisor chose Student B as the "Employee of the Month." The employee feels very uncomfortable and asks the supervisor to take down the photograph. The supervisor thinks that it is an honor to be "Employee of the Month" and doesn't want to take down the photograph. Act out what happens.

2. Student A is a new employee in a small office. Student A is shy and doesn't seem friendly. Students B and C began working together in the office three years ago, and they now are very good friends. They do many things together both at work and after work. They think that Student A is unfriendly. Student A feels alone and uncomfortable at work. This is affecting Student A's work performance. Student D is the supervisor. The supervisor notices that Student A's work performance is not very good. When the supervisor talks to Student A, the supervisor finds out about the situation and decides to try to do something about it. Act out what happens.

Activity 2: Brainstorming *(expressing opinions, identifying characteristics of good workers)*

A. With a partner, list five characteristics of a good co-worker.

1. hard-working _____

2. _____

3. _____

4. _____

5. _____

Compare your list with your class. Which characteristics were the same? Which ones were different? How many characteristics were there altogether?

B.   With your partner, list five characteristics of a good supervisor.

1. _good listener_ _____

2. _____

3. _____

4. _____

5. _____

Compare your list with your class. Which characteristics were the same? Which ones were different? How many characteristics were there altogether?

Activity 3 *(relating topic to actual work situations)*

Discuss these questions in class:

1.   Why is it important to get along with your co-workers?
2.   Is it necessary to like all of your co-workers?
3.   What do you do when another worker isn't doing his or her job?
4.   How can you develop a good relationship with your supervisor?
5.   Do you need to like your supervisor in order to develop a good relationship with him or her?
6.   What can you do if you have a problem with your supervisor?

Reading at Work

Understanding New Words
(expanding vocabulary, understanding new words through context)

Read the sentences below. Find and circle the underlined words in the reading that follows.

1.   Our <u>work behavior</u> is how we act at work.
2.   People <u>exhibit</u> or show different personality characteristics.
3.   Some people like to <u>take charge</u> or take control of a situation.
4.   Employers look for workers with good <u>interpersonal skills</u>. Employers look for employees with the ability to work well with other people.
5.   Sammy and Tom try to <u>get things done</u> on time. They try to accomplish or finish their tasks on time.
6.   It's important to <u>stick with</u> or continue to work hard at a problem until you can find a solution.

Our personalities affect how we do our job and how we work with others. Sometimes companies want workers to think about their personalities, so that the employees can understand themselves and others better. One company gives its employees the following information about personality characteristics.

One way that we can understand ourselves and our co-workers better is to learn about work behavior styles. There are four basic styles.

Dominance—People who exhibit this style like to take charge. They obtain the results that they want because they try to control the situation.

Influencing—People who exhibit this style use their interpersonal skills. They get the results that they want because they get other people to help them.

Steadiness—People who exhibit this style have a lot of patience. They get things done because they stick with their tasks and cooperate with others.

Compliance—People who exhibit this work style try to achieve high quality in their work. They get things done because they follow directions and take care of important details.

Everyone has some elements of all four styles in his or her work behavior. However, one style is usually more noticeable than the others.

Understanding the Reading

(relating reading to work experiences)

Answer the following questions in class.

1. Why is it important for you to understand something about your personality?
2. How can understanding your own personality help you to enjoy your job more?
3. What are some ways that your personality can have a positive effect on your job?
4. Look at the cartoon. What does it show? What does it mean?

PERSONALITIES OFTEN GET LEFT OUTSIDE

PUT PERSONALITY INTO YOUR WORK

Listening

(listening for specific information, filling in a chart)

Mrs. Sims is introducing her new employee, Mark, to the other food service workers. Listen to what she says and write the names below in the appropriate boxes.

Beverly	Michiko	Ms. Black
Juan	Mr. Ned Anderson	Robert
Linda	Mr. Bill Anderson	Sammy
Loretta	Mr. Ortiz	Tom
Mark	✔ Mrs. Sims	Tony

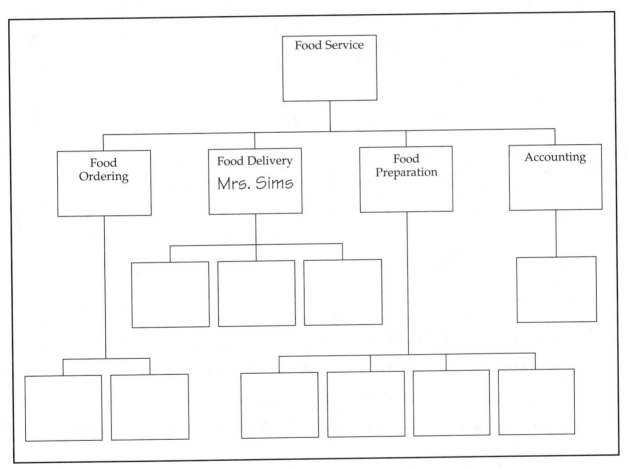

Using Math and Reading a Table
(reading and interpreting a table, multiplying decimals, filling in a table)

Ivan and Jack work as a team at the ABC Steel Company. They need to cut 100,000 bars of steel a day. If they cut more than 100,000 bars, they receive an incentive (extra money). The incentive depends on *how many extra bars* they cut and on *what kinds of bars* they cut. Look at the table below and answer the questions.

Incentives for Steel Cutting at ABC Steel Company						
Units Per 1,000	Bar #1	Bar #2	Bar #3	Bar #4	Bar #5	Bar #6
1	$0.80	$1.00	$1.50	$0.50	$0.75	$1.20
2	1.60	2.00	3.00	1.00	1.50	2.40
3	2.40	3.00	4.50	1.50	2.25	3.60
4	3.20	4.00	6.00	2.00	3.00	4.80
5	4.00	5.00		2.50	3.75	6.00
6			9.00		4.50	
7	5.60	7.00		3.50		8.40
8			12.00		6.00	
9	7.20					
10				5.00		12.00

1. How many different kinds of bars are there? _____

2. Which bar (per 1,000) do Ivan and Jack receive the most money for? _____

3. Which bar (per 1,000) do they receive the least money for? _____

4. How much incentive do they receive for making 3,000 extra of Bar #3?

    _____

5. How much is their incentive when they make 5,000 extra of Bar #6?

    _____

6. Do they receive more incentive for making 6,000 extra of Bar #5 or 5,000

    extra of Bar #1? _____

7. Do they receive more incentive for making 8,000 extra of Bar #3 than they

    receive for making 10,000 extra of Bar #6? _____

8. Complete the table. (*Hint:* To finish the table, multiply the incentive for each bar by the number of units. For example, if the incentive is $1.50 (Bar #3) and the number of units is 5, then Ivan and Jack will make $1.50 x 5 = $7.50 for each 5,000 extra bars that they cut.)

Writing
(expanding vocabulary, expressing feelings, completing sentences)

Talk about the meanings of these words.

angry	dependable	pressured
annoyed	frustrated	proud
capable	furious	relieved
confident	happy	responsible
confused	nervous	satisfied

Use six of the words to complete the following sentences.

0. I am _____proud_____ when _____I do a good job_____.

1. I am _____ when _____.

2. I feel _____ when _____.

3. My co-workers are _____ when _____.

4. My co-workers feel _____ when _____.

5. My supervisor is _____ when _____.

6. My supervisor feels _____ when _____.

UNIT 7   *Valued Work Behaviors*

Before You Read
(making predictions, relating experiences to reading, establishing prior knowledge)

Cathy

Talk about this comic strip with a partner.

Write your answers on the lines.

1. Where is Cathy?_____

2. What is she trying to do? _____

3. What's the problem with the coffeepot? _____

4. Why is Cathy mad?_____

5. Do you work on a crew or team, or do you work alone? _____

 _____

6. If you work on a crew or team, how do your co-workers depend on you?

 _____

Reading About Work

Hamburger Heaven Helpers

"One Coke, a large order of fries, and one burger—no onions," the man said as he scanned the list of food at Hamburger Heaven. "Coming right up, sir," Ali answered cheerfully. He spoke into the microphone, "One Coke, one large fries, one burger, no onions."

Then Ali asked himself, "Why did I say 'One Coke?' Hal's job is to get the drinks, but he isn't here today. I'll have to get the Coke." He carefully filled the cup with Coke and placed it on the tray.

Ali called to Kenji, "How about the fries?" Kenji answered, "Almost ready." Pedro handed the hamburger to Ali and said, "I'll be glad when we can go home tonight. Our new advertisement, 'Your meal in under three minutes or it's free,' puts a lot of pressure on us, especially when we're short a person. We really need Hal today to fill the drink orders. Now I understand why Mr. Gupta stresses teamwork. It's more work when a member of the team is missing."

Kenji arrived with the fries. Ali took the customer's money, and gave the customer his change. Mr. Gupta, the manager, joined the group at the cash register. He said, "What a busy day! I have some good news and some bad news for you. The good news is there's only half an hour to closing time. The bad news is there's an emergency at my home. I need to leave now."

"Who's going to take the money to the bank?" asked Pedro.

"Well, I'm going to need your help tonight," answered Mr. Gupta. "Ali, you're the team leader. I'm putting you in charge. You need to count the money in the register. Then fill out a deposit slip and take the money to the night deposit at the American National Bank. Take Pedro and Kenji with you. It's safer to go in a group. I almost never let my employees deposit the money, but the three of you are always very honest and pleasant with the customers. Your attitude is certainly one reason that we're so busy! I'm glad that I have such a hard-working, trustworthy team of employees!"

Understanding New Words and Phrases
(expanding vocabulary, understanding new words through context)

Read these sentences with a partner. Decide together if *a* or *b* means the same as the underlined words in the sentence. Circle *a* or *b*.

1. "One Coke, a large order of fries and one burger—no onions," the man said as he <u>scanned</u> the list of food.

    a. looked quickly

    b. studied carefully

2. "Our new advertisement, 'Your meal in under three minutes or it's free,' <u>puts a lot of pressure on us</u>."

    a. makes our job easy and fast

    b. makes us anxious and worried

3. "<u>We're short a person.</u>"

    a. One person is shorter than the others.

    b. We need one more person to have a complete team.

4. "Now I understand why Mr. Gupta <u>stresses</u> working as a team."

    a. talks about the importance of

    b. shouts about

5. "Ali, <u>I'm putting you in charge</u>."

    a. I'm making you the supervisor.

    b. I'm letting you go home early.

6. "I'm glad that I have such a hard-working, <u>trustworthy</u> team of employees."

    a. fast-working

    b. dependable and honest

Understanding the Reading

(checking literal and inferential comprehension)

Fill in the box that answers the question.

1. Where do Ali, Pedro, Kenji, and Hal work?

    ☐ at an Italian restaurant

    ■ at a hamburger stand

    ☐ at a hospital

2. How long is the restaurant open?

    ☐ 24 hours

    ☐ less than 24 hours

3. How quickly does the team need to serve the customer's meal?

    ☐ in more than three minutes

    ☐ in less than one minute

    ☐ in less than three minutes

4. Which worker is absent?

    ☐ Mr. Gupta's wife

    ☐ Hal

    ☐ Kenji

5. Who makes the fries?

    ☐ Kenji

    ☐ Hal

    ☐ Ali

6. At the end of the day, what happens to the money?

    ☐ Mr. Gupta keeps it at the restaurant.

    ☐ Mr. Gupta takes it to a bank.

    ☐ Mr. Gupta takes it home.

7. Why does Mr. Gupta need to leave early?

    ☐ There's an emergency at his home.

    ☐ He's tired.

    ☐ He needs to deposit the money.

8. How often does Mr. Gupta let his employees deposit the money?

    ☐ always

    ☐ usually

    ☐ almost never

Discussing
(synthesizing information, making inferences, completing a chart, problem solving)

Making a Work Schedule

Each week, Mr. Gupta makes a work schedule for his employees. Help him make the schedule for Kenji, Hal, Ali, and Pedro. The three shifts are:

> 10–4   (Every day)
>   2–8   (Sunday, Monday, Tuesday, Wednesday, Thursday)
> 4–10   (Friday and Saturday)

Form a team and use the information below to determine the schedules for the four workers. Fill in the following chart after you read the information.

	S	M	T	W	Th	F	Sa
Ali		10–4		✗			
Hal							
Kenji							
Pedro							

Ali is the team leader. He works six days (36 hours). He has Wednesday off. He opens the restaurant only on Mondays and Tuesdays. He closes the restaurant four days a week.

Hal works five days (30 hours). He has Monday and Saturday off. He opens the restaurant only on Tuesday. He closes the restaurant four days a week.

Kenji works five days (30 hours). He has Sunday and Thursday off. He opens the restaurant on Monday and Tuesday. He closes the restaurant the other days that he works.

Pedro works four days (24 hours). He works the same schedule as Ali, Hal, and Kenji on Tuesday and Friday. He works on the same shift with Ali and Hal on Sunday. He works with Ali and Kenji on Saturday.

Use the completed chart to answer the following questions.

1. On which days does Mr. Gupta have a complete team (four workers) for one shift? _____

2. On which days does Mr. Gupta need to add one more employee to form a team? _____

3. On which days does Mr. Gupta need to add two more employees to form a team? _____

Reading at Work

Understanding New Words
(expanding vocabulary, understanding new words through context)

Read the sentences below. Find and circle the underlined words in the reading that follows.

1. The number of customers at Hamburger Heaven is <u>growing</u>. The number of customers is getting bigger.
2. A <u>dishonest</u> person is not trustworthy. A dishonest person may steal or not tell the truth.
3. Employee dishonesty is a <u>concern</u>, or something that many employers worry about.

The Tasty Cookie Company is having problems with dishonest employees. Some employees are stealing boxes of cookies. Read the following letter sent to all employees.

No one at the Tasty Cookie Company likes to think that a co-worker is dishonest, and not many employees are dishonest. But the truth is that dishonest employees are a growing concern. It's normal for an honest employee to feel uncomfortable telling a supervisor about a co-worker who is stealing. However, it's our company and when the Tasty Cookie Company loses, we all lose. All of us work very hard. Dishonest employees hurt the company and affect the attitude of honest, trustworthy employees.

Understanding the Reading
(checking literal comprehension, relating the reading to work experiences)

Answer the following questions about the reading.

1. What is a growing problem at the Tasty Cookie Company?
2. How do honest employees feel about telling supervisors about dishonest employees?
3. Explain: It's our company and when the Tasty Cookie Company loses, we all lose.
4. Trustworthy means not stealing. What other examples of being trustworthy on the job can you think of?

Listening

(listening for specific information [numbers], working on teams to synthesize information, filling in a chart, using math)

Mr. Gupta, the manager of Hamburger Heaven, wants to find out how much money his restaurant made during one Monday–Friday workweek. His restaurant makes bank deposits after each meal, so there are three deposits each day. This week Mr. Gupta has a problem. He didn't put all of the deposit slips in one place. He is looking for the deposit slips, which are in *three* different places.

Before you listen to the tape, your teacher will help you to form teams. There will be three people on a team. Each member of the team is going to hear one part of the tape. Each team member will then be able to fill in one third of the table below. After all team members have heard their parts of the tape, each team will combine their information to finish the table.

Table of Monday–Friday Bank Deposits for Hamburger Heaven

	Monday	Tuesday	Wednesday	Thursday	Friday
Breakfast					
Lunch					
Dinner					

After you finish the table with your teammates, answer the following questions.

1. Which lunch made the most money? _____

2. Which breakfast made the most money? _____

3. Which dinner made the most money? _____

4. Which day was the best for Hamburger Heaven? _____

5. Which day was second best? _____

6. Which day made the least money? _____

7. How much money did Hamburger Heaven make during the week? _____

Using Circle Graphs
(reading and interpreting a circle graph, identifying percentages)

Between 12:00 and 1:00 each day, each Hamburger Heaven restaurant offers an "express meal" consisting of one jumbo hamburger, one order of small fries, and one medium soft drink. There are six Hamburger Heaven restaurants in Middletown, U.S.A.

Below is a *circle graph*, which shows the total number of express meals served at all six Hamburger Heaven restaurants on one day. Each section of the circle graph represents the number of express meals that each Hamburger Heaven restaurant sold.

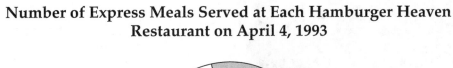

Number of Express Meals Served at Each Hamburger Heaven Restaurant on April 4, 1993

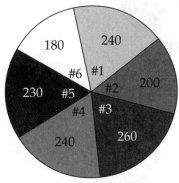

Look at the circle graph. Read the title. Then answer the questions.

1. Which day does this circle graph refer to? _____

2. Which restaurant served the most express meals?_____

3. Which restaurant served the fewest express meals? _____

4. Which restaurant served more express meals—restaurant #4 or #5? _____

5. What is the total number of express meals served at all six of the

   Hamburger Heaven restaurants? _____

We can also express the numbers on the circle graph in percentages (parts of 100 that add up to 100). Match the percentages below to the number of express meals that are sold and finish the circle graph.

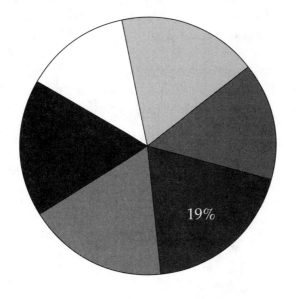

19%	_260_
18%	_____
18%	_____
17%	_____
15%	_____
13%	_____
100%	_____

(This number is the same as the answer to #5 on page 81.)

What began with a few pencils and paper clips . . .

Writing

(using context clues and creative thinking to complete a conversation)

Look at the cartoons on the left and decide what is happening in each picture. Then look at the partial (not finished) conversations on the right. Decide what each person is saying. Write complete conversations in the correct balloons.

a. "Sorry, Josef. I was talking to a friend. _____

_____

_____ "

b. "Thank you for returning Sam's paycheck, Ernesto.

_____

_____

_____ "

c. "Hey, Mike. Let's get back to work. We're a team, right?

_____

_____

_____ "

d. "You're welcome, Mr. Cole. I know that Sam has a family.

_____

_____

_____ "

UNIT 8 *Job Performance*

Before You Read
(making predictions, relating experiences to reading, establishing prior knowledge)

Talk about this drawing with a partner.

Write your answers on the lines.

1. Why is Mr. Perry unhappy? _____

2. What does he want? _____

    _____

3. How can Mr. Perry's workers help him meet his goal? _____

    _____

Reading About Work

Elsa Comes Through

Mr. Yang walked over to Elsa's desk. "Elsa," he said, "I have rush job for you. I know that I can count on you to finish it before 4:00 today. That gives you two hours to work on the job. This is what I want you to do. Here are five reports from my assistant managers. The reports contain information about defective parts. And this other paper is my summary of the reports. I want you to type the five reports and my summary, too. Be careful—there are lot of numbers!" Elsa said, "I'll start working on it right away." Mr. Yang continued, "Remember, I have to send out the final report today at 4:00. Sorry about the short notice."

Elsa scanned the reports, and then she looked at Mr. Yang's summary. She made her job easier and faster because she had good idea of what she needed to do. She studied Mr. Yang's summary, and she noticed that his numbers didn't match the numbers on the fourth report. She decided to check with Mr. Yang, but he wasn't in his office. Elsa said to herself, "I'll have to work around this problem. I can't finish the report until I talk to Mr. Yang. I'll work on the other reports. I'll hold off on the fourth report and the summary until Mr. Yang comes back."

Elsa was busy at her desk when Mr. Yang walked into the office. She called to him, "Mr. Yang, I have question about the summary." He looked at the report and said, "Elsa, I'm glad that I you noticed this. I made some mistakes. Here are the corrections. Can you finish this in half an hour?" Elsa answered, "Yes, I finished the other reports. This is the last thing I need to do. It will be on your desk by 4:00. "Mr. Yang smiled, "Thanks for being speedy and for being *so* accurate."

Understanding New Words

(expanding vocabulary, understanding new words through context)

Read these sentences with a partner. Decide together if sentence *a* or *b* means the same as the sentence in the reading. Circle *a* or *b*.

1. Mr. Yang said to Elsa, "I have a <u>rush job</u> for you."

   a. "I need you to do a job quickly."
   b. "I need you to run to the store for me."

2. "And this other paper is my <u>summary</u> of the reports."

   a. "And this other paper contains only the principal ideas of the reports."
   b. "And this other paper contains new information about the reports."

3. "Sorry about the <u>short notice</u>."

   a. "Sorry about the small quantity of news."
   b. "Sorry about telling you only a little time before."

4. "The reports contain information about <u>defective parts</u>."'

   a. "The reports contain information about parts that don't work correctly."
   b. "The reports contain information about extra parts."

5. "I'll have to <u>work around</u> this problem."

   a. "I'll have to concentrate on something else for a while before I consider this problem."
   b. "I'll have to concentrate on this problem immediately."

6. "I'll <u>hold off</u> on the fourth report."

   a. "I'll put the fourth report in my hand."
   b. "I'll wait awhile before I do the fourth report."

Understanding the Reading

(identifying details, checking literal and inferential comprehension)

A. TRUE/FALSE: Read these sentences with a partner. Decide together if they are *true* or *false*. Circle *T* for true and *F* for false.

    1. The reports contain information about employees' salaries.   *T   F*

    2. It is 1:00 at the beginning of the reading.   *T   F*

    3. Mr. Yang's summary is correct.   *T   F*

    4. Elsa decides to hold off on the fifth report.   *T   F*

    5. Elsa is working under pressure.   *T   F*

    6. Elsa works for an hour and half before Mr. Yang returns.   *T   F*

    7. Mr. Yang is happy that Elsa notices his mistake.   *T   F*

    8. Elsa is an accurate and fast worker.   *T   F*

B. There are four *false* sentences in Exercise A. Rewrite the false sentences to make them true.

    1. _____

    2. _____

    3. _____

    4. _____

Discussing

Activity 1: Checking for accuracy *(proofreading, scanning for specific information)*

Linda is a new clerk typist at BMI Computer Company. Mr. Yang gave her a summary to type, but she made a lot of mistakes. Work with a partner. Look at Mr. Yang's summary. Then look at Linda's typewritten summary. Try to find 18 errors in two minutes. Your instructor will tell you when to start.

DEFECTIVE PARTS FOR MONTHS OF JAN.–AUG. 1992

PART #→	10045B	21003P	46018D	59367F	39002C	76234Z
MONTH ↓						
JAN.	15	21	6	3	21	13
FEB.	10	5	11	12	8	3
MAR.	2	14	17	9	16	10
APR.	9	35	4	13	17	5
MAY	4	18	2	12	21	14
JUN.	0	7	11	32	23	9
JUL.	3	15	24	18	11	31
AUG.	17	23	16	22	14	7

DEFECTIVE PARTS FOR MONTHS OF JUN.–AUG. 1992

PART# ->	10045P	21003B	4608D	59367F	39002Z	76233Z
MONTH ↓						
JAN.	15	12	6	3	21	31
FEB.	10	5	12	11	8	3
MAR.	2	14	17	9	16	10
MAR.	2	35	4	31	17	5
MAY	4	18	2	12	21	14
JUN.	0	7	11	32	23	9
JUL.	3	7	24	18	11	31
AGU.	71	23	61	22	41	7

Activity 2: Role play *(using critical thinking in role plays, empathizing with a character)*

Student A is Mr. Yang. Student B is Linda. Mr. Yang needs to talk to Linda about her typing. He is worried about her job performance. He tells Linda that she makes too many mistakes and she needs to be more careful. Linda tries to be a good employee, and she knows that she makes too many mistakes. However, she is very sensitive and does not like criticism.

Activity 3 *(relating topic to actual work situations, predicting consequences)*

Discuss these questions in class.

1. Why is it important to be accurate on your job?
2. Is speed important on your job? Why or why not?
3. Do you need to be both fast and accurate on your job?
4. What happens if you make a mistake?
5. What happens if you don't work fast enough?

Reading at Work

Here is an article from a company newsletter. It explains how the performance of *each* employee is important to the company. Be careful when you read! The typewriter wasn't very accurate!

THINK THIS ONX OVXR

My typxwritxr is an old modxl. It works quitx wxll, xxcxpt for onx kxy. It's trux that thxrx arx 41 kxys that function wxll xnough, but just onx kxy makxs thx diffxrxncx. Thxrx arx timxs whxn a company is somxwhat likx my typxwritxr— not all thx pxoplx arx working propxrly. You may say to yoursxlf, "I can't makx or brxak my company." But you do makx a diffxrxncx!! A company nxxds thx activx participation of all its xmployxxs. So thx nxxt timx you think your xfforts arxn't nxxdxd, just rxmxmbxr my typxwritxr and say to yoursxlf: I am a kxy pxrson in my company, and I'm nxxdxd vxry much.

Understanding the Reading

(checking literal comprehension, relating reading to work experience)

Answer these questions in class.

1. How many keys on the typewriter work properly?
2. Which key doesn't work properly?
3. How does that key make a difference?
4. How is a company like a typewriter?
5. How is an employee of a company a "key" person?
6. How is your job performance important to your company?

Listening

(listening to verify specific information, problem solving)

Listen to the tape. You will hear descriptions of how employees performed their jobs. Read the checklist and decide if the employee in each situation performed the job correctly. Put check (✔) under *Yes* or *No*.

Making Fries at Hamburger Heaven

		Yes	No
1.	Heat oil to 335°.	✔	
2.	Fill baskets one-third full with potatoes.		
3.	Put fry basket into hot oil.		
4.	Turn on fry computer.		
5.	Take basket out of oil when buzzer sounds.		
6.	Drain fries for five seconds.		
7.	Salt fries.		
8.	Throw away cooked fries after five minutes.		

Taking Orders at Hamburger Heaven

		Yes	No
1.	Smile and greet customer.	____	____
2.	Listen to order and repeat it into microphone.	____	____
3.	Enter orders into cash register.	____	____
4.	If order is not clear, repeat it to customer.	____	____
5.	Ring total on cash register.	____	____
6.	Tell customer the total amount of money he needs to pay.	____	____
7.	Take customer's money and put it on top of cash register drawer when you need to make change.	____	____
8.	Count change as you give it to customer.	____	____
9.	Check order for accuracy before giving it to customer.	____	____
10.	Thank customer.	____	____

Assembling Dolls at Favorite Toys Company

		Yes	No
1.	Fit Part A into Part B.	____	____
2.	Fit Part C into Part D.	____	____
3.	Fit Part E into Part F.	____	____
4.	Fit Part G into Part H.	____	____
5.	Fit Part I into Part J.	____	____
6.	Assemble at least one doll every minute.	____	____

Making Beds at Eastlake Hospital

		Yes	No
1.	Load cart in supply room.	____	____
2.	Take 200 sheets.	____	____
3.	Take 100 pillowcases.	____	____
4.	Take 100 blankets.	____	____
5.	Finish at least 50 rooms (two beds in each room) in 4½ hours.	____	____

Reading a Graph
(reading and interpreting a line graph)

The BMI Computer Company makes computer chips. Computer chips are small electronic pieces that make computers work. Every hour, the employees at BMI need to make a certain number of chips, but they cannot make too many defective ones. Look at the graph below, and then write the answers to the questions.

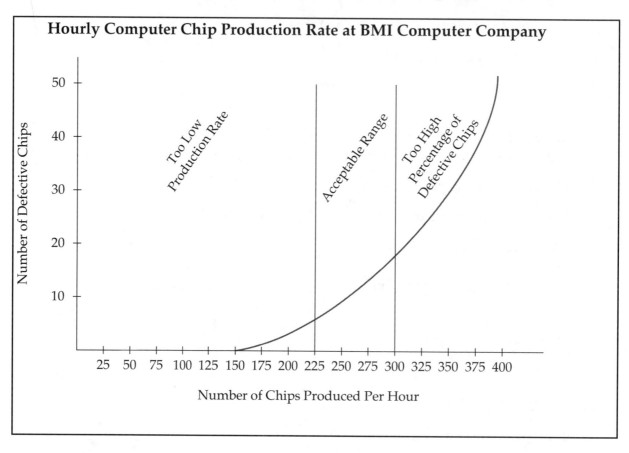

1. What do the numbers on the left side of the graph show? _____

    _____

2. What do the numbers on the bottom of the graph show? _____

    _____

3. What is the minimum acceptable number of chips produced per hour?

    _____ What is the maximum number of defective chips allowed

    at this point? _____

4. According to this graph, at what point are too many defective chips

    produced?_____

5. Is it acceptable if a worker produces 200 chips per hour with no defective ones? _____

6. Is it acceptable if a worker produces 250 chips per hour with 10 defective ones? _____

7. Is it acceptable if a worker produces 350 chips in an hour with 30 defective ones? _____

Writing

(using context clues to determine missing vowels)

Mr. Yang typed Elsa's job evaluation on his typewriter at home. However, the vowel keys (*a,e,* and *o*) on his typewriter don't work. Fill in the missing vowels in the evaluation as quickly and accurately as you can.

<u>E v a lu a ti o n</u>   <u>o f</u>   <u>E ls a</u>   <u>Jo hns o n</u>

<u>E ls a</u>   h__s   w__rk__d   __s   __   typist   in   my   __ffic__   f__r   six

m__nths.   Sh__   l____rn__d   h__r   j__b   v__ry   quickly,   __nd   sh__   is   __n

__xc__ll__nt   w__rk__r.   Sh__   is   __lw__ys   __n   tim__,   __nd   sh__   is

__lm__st   n__v__r   __bs__nt.   It   is   v__ry   imp__rt__nt   f__r   __   typist   t__

b__   f__st   __nd   __ccur__t__.   __ls__   is   b__th!   Sh__   is   v__ry   sp____dy

__nd   __lm__st   n__v__r   m__k__s   mist__k__s.   Sh__   ch__cks   h__r   w__rk,

__nd   sh__   __sks   qu__sti__ns   wh__n   sh__'s   n__t   sur__   __b__ut

s__m__thing.   Sh__   is   __ls__   v__ry   g____d   __t   m__th.   This   is

imp__rt__nt   b__c__us__   p__rt   __f   h__r   j__b   is   typing   __nd   ch__cking

m__th   pr__bl__ms.   __ls__   is   __   v__ry   r__sp__nsibl__   p__rs__n   __nd   is

l____rning   t__   m__k__   d__cisi__ns   __n   th__   j__b.   Sh__   h__s   __ll   th__

qu__liti__s   th__t   I   l____k   f__r   in   __   g____d   __mpl__y____!

UNIT 9 *Goal Setting*

Before You Read
(making predictions, relating experiences to reading, establishing prior knowledge)

Credit: Frank Siteman/Stock, Boston

Talk about this photograph with a partner.

Write your answers on the lines.

1. Where is this person? _____

2. What is she doing? _____

3. Why is she looking at the bulletin board? _____

_____

4. If you want a different job at your company, what steps do you need to

take? _____

_____

Reading About Work

Ida's Plans

Ida and Ahmed were walking to their machines on the factory floor. Ida was telling Ahmed about the job opening for supervisor that she saw on the company bulletin board. "I'm going to apply for the position," she told Ahmed. "I'll make $1.50 an hour more, and I can go on the day shift. And that means that I can take a class at the community college at night. I want to learn about computers. I hope someday to get an office job here." "You certainly have a lot of plans," Ahmed said. "You're set for the next five years!"

At 3:00 the next afternoon, Ida went to talk to Mr. Henderson, the personnel manager. Mr. Henderson looked at her application. "Ida, you're one of my best machine operators. You're a very conscientious worker, and I know that you want the supervisor's job. But, we need to look at things realistically. I see that you started working here just two years ago. Some of the other applicants for the supervisor's job started working here five to ten years ago. It's also very important to have experience on all of the machines. How many machines do you know how to operate?" Ida answered, "I know how to operate three in my section, but I don't have any experience in other departments."

"Knowledge of all the machines is necessary to be a supervisor, Ida," Mr. Henderson told her. "There are other applicants with more experience and knowledge. I can't give you the supervisor's job now, but I know that you want to change to the day shift. I'll put you on the day shift, and you'll learn how to operate one of the new machines. That will give you more experience. When more openings come up in the future, you'll be better prepared to be a supervisor."

Ida was happy. "If I go on the day shift, I can take a night class at college. And I'll learn something new at work. I'll have the best of both worlds!"

Understanding New Words and Idioms

(expanding vocabulary, understanding new words through context)

Read these sentences with a partner. Decide together if sentence *a* or *b* means the same as the sentence in the reading. Circle *a* or *b*.

1.   "I can take a class at the <u>community college</u>."

   a. "I can take a class at a two-year college."
   b. "I can take a class at a four-year college."

2.   "<u>You're set</u> for the next five years!"

   a. "You don't need any more plans for the next five years."
   b. "You will sit down for the next five years."

3.   "Ida, I know that you're a very <u>conscientious</u> worker."

   a. "I know that you're not a very good worker."
   b. "I know that you're a very careful and serious worker."

4.   "We need to look at things <u>realistically</u>."

   a. "We need to look at things the way we want them to be."
   b. "We need to look at things the way they are."

5.   "<u>Knowledge</u> of all the machines is necessary to be a supervisor."

   a. "It is necessary to know how to operate all the machines to be a supervisor."
   b. "The ability to repair all the machines is necessary to be a supervisor."

6.   "When more openings <u>come up</u> in the future, you'll be better prepared."

   a. "When there are more openings in the future, you'll be better prepared."
   b. "When you take more classes, you'll be better prepared."

Understanding the Reading

(checking literal comprehension)

Matching: Work with a partner. Match the words in Part A and Part B to make sentences. Then write the sentences on the lines.

Part A	Part B
1. Ida saw an opening for	all of the machines in the department.
2. Mr. Henderson said that Ida is	a job on the day shift.
3. Ida knows how to operate	had more knowledge and experience than Ida.
4. To be a supervisor, a person needs to be familiar with	she didn't have enough knowledge and experience.
5. Mr. Henderson didn't give Ida the job because	a supervisor's job in her company.
6. Mr. Henderson gave Ida	a very conscientious worker.
7. Mr. Henderson said that other employees	she will learn how to operate a new machine, and she can go to school.
8. After talking to Mr. Henderson Ida was happy because	three machines in her section.

1. _____

_____

2. _____

3. _____

4. _____

5. _____

6. _____

7. _____

8. _____

_____

Discussing
(expressing opinions, evaluating reasons, making judgments)

Activity 1: Setting realistic goals

Look at the following goals with a partner. Decide if they are realistic goals. Check
(✔) *Yes, No,* or *Maybe.*

	Yes	No	Maybe
1. Learning how to operate a new machine in your department.	____	____	____
2. Receiving a $.50–$1.00 raise within the next year.	____	____	____
3. Taking one training course and earning $5.00 more an hour than you earn now.	____	____	____
4. Taking one basic math course and knowing all of the math you will need to know in your lifetime.	____	____	____
5. Planning to take no more than one or two training courses in a year.	____	____	____
6. Planning to be a supervisor one year after starting a job.	____	____	____
7. Understanding the need for more education and planning a schedule to take courses.	____	____	____
8. Talking to your boss to find out what you will need to do to get a promotion.	____	____	____

Activity 2: Ordering *(sequencing and prioritizing information)*

Lin works at BMI Computer Company. He's a packer, but he wants to be a computer programmer. Following is a list of things he needs to do to reach his goal. Decide in which order Lin needs to do them. Put number *1* next to what he'll do first, number *2* next to what he'll do second, and so on.

_____ Save money for school.

_____ Decide to talk to supervisor about promotion.

_____ Find out about course or courses that he needs to take.

_____ Decide what kind of job in the company he wants.

_____ Register for course.

_____ Talk to an advisor at the community college.

_____ Take course or courses.

_____ Apply for promotion.

Activity 3: Interview *(interviewing, reporting information)*

Interview your partner about his or her goals. Take notes and then tell the class about your partner's goals.

1. When did you start working here?_____

2. What were your duties? _____

3. What is your job now? _____

4. How did you get the job that you have now?_____

    _____

5. Do you plan to stay in your present job or do you plan to get a promotion?

    _____

6. If you plan to get a promotion, what kind of job do you want? _____

    _____

7. How do you plan to do this? _____

8. When do you plan to do this? _____

9. Is this your final goal? _____

Reading at Work

Understanding New Words
(expanding vocabulary, understanding new words through context)

Read the sentences below. Find and circle the underlined words in the reading.

1. <u>Shoplifting</u> is when people take items from stores without paying.

2. Stores want to <u>cut down on</u>, or decrease, shoplifting.

3. A <u>short-term goal</u> is one that we hope to reach in the near future.

4. A <u>long-term goal</u> is one that we hope to reach in the distant future.

People have goals for themselves, and companies also have goals. The following reading describes one of the goals of Doyle's Department Store.

Shoplifting is a big concern in our store. It costs the store and our customers a lot of extra money. Doyle's is trying very hard to cut down on the amount of shoplifting in our store, but we need everyone's help! We have about 120 cases of shoplifting every month. Our short-term goal is to decrease the number of cases to only one case a day. Of course, *no* shoplifting is our long-term goal! We need the help of all of our employees to reach our goal. *You* can help keep our costs down. Keep your eyes open and report all shoplifters!

Understanding the Reading
(checking literal comprehension, relating reading to work situations)

Answer the following questions in class.

1. Why is shoplifting a big concern at Doyle's?
2. Approximately how many cases of shoplifting does Doyle's have every day?
3. What is Doyle's short-term goal?
4. What is Doyle's long-term goal?
5. How can employees help Doyle's to cut down on shoplifting?
6. What short-term and long-term goals does your company have?

Listening

Activity 1: Filling in times and days of the week *(listening for specific information)*

Listen to the tape. You will hear a description of Ida's activities during one week. On the list below, fill in the time and the days that she does the activities.

		Time	Day(s) of Week
1.	Gets up	6:00	M–F
2.	Washes clothes	6:00	M–F
3.	Makes breakfast	7:00	M–F
4.	Takes daughter to day care		
5.	Takes son to school		
6.	Starts work		
7.	Finishes work		
8.	Picks up daughter at day care		
9.	Picks up son at neighbor's house		
10.	Makes supper		
11.	Bought a birthday present and card for co-worker		
12.	Went to library to study for test		
13.	Went to computer class		
14.	Went to post office and cleaners		
15.	Went to computer lab		
16.	Left work early to go to conference at son's school		
17.	Went to Diamond Foods		
18.	Met with supervisor		
19.	Took family to Hamburger Heaven for supper		

Activity 2: Filling in a table (*figuring out a schedule, filling in a table*)

Use the information from Activity 1 to fill in Ida's schedule for one week.

TIME	DAYS OF THE WEEK				
	Monday	Tuesday	Wednesday	Thursday	Friday
6:00 A.M.			Gets Up / Washes Clothes		
7:00 A.M.			Makes Breakfast		
8:00 A.M.					
9:00 A.M.					
10:00 A.M.					
11:00 A.M.					
12:00 NOON					
1:00 P.M.					
2:00 P.M.					
3:00 P.M.					
4:00 P.M.					
5:00 P.M.					
6:00 P.M.					
7:00 P.M.					
8:00 P.M.					
9:00 P.M.					
10:00 P.M.					

Reading a Graph

Activity 1: Reading a picture graph *(reading and interpreting a picture graph)*

Following is a *picture graph*. It shows two things: how many people at the Excel Corporation are taking classes and which classes they are taking. Look at the graph and answer the questions.

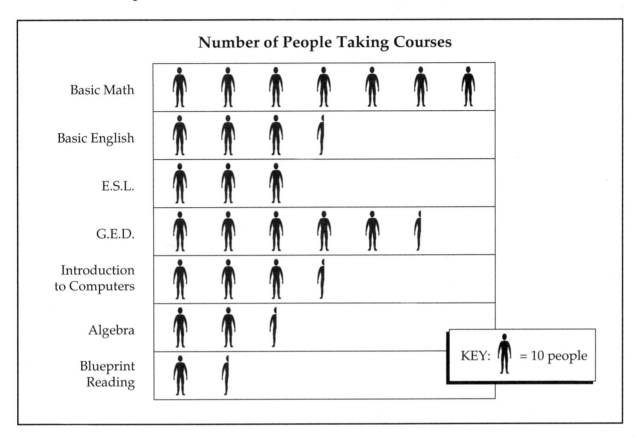

Number of People Taking Courses

KEY: 📍 = 10 people

1. What is on the left side of the graph?_____

2. What does the *key* show? _____

3. How many people are taking a basic math course?_____

4. How many people are taking an E.S.L. course? _____

5. Are more people taking a G.E.D. course or an algebra course?_____

   _____

6. Which course has the most students? _____

7. Which course has the fewest students? _____

Activity 2: Making a bar graph *(interpreting information from one graph to make another graph)*

Use the information from the picture graph to complete the *bar graph* below.

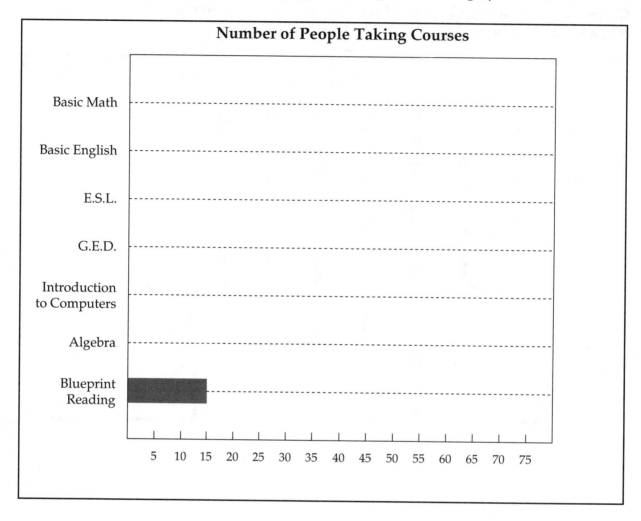

Writing
(synthesizing information, writing a paragraph expressing goals)

Look again at the questions in Activity 3 in *Discussing*. Write *your* answers to the questions in paragraph form. Below are Ida's answers in paragraph form.

    I started to work at this company two years ago. I started as a machine operator. I am still a machine operator, but I know how to operate three different machines in my department. I have the same title, but I received a pay raise each time that I learned a new machine. I trained on the new machines to get the job that I have now. I plan to stay in my present job for a while because I just started on the day shift. I am learning how to operate one of the new machines in my department. I am very happy with my present job. I plan to get a promotion later—after I learn how to operate the other machines in the department. I hope to be a supervisor in the next two years. I will also need to take some training courses on how to be a supervisor. My long-term goal is to work in the office of this company. This goal will take some time! Right now I am taking a computer course at the community college. I will need to take other courses, too. The counselor at the community college will help me choose the courses that I need. Someday I will reach my goal!

_____

_____

_____

_____

_____

_____

_____

_____

_____

_____

_____

_____

UNIT 10 *Job Training/Continuing Education*

Before You Read
(making predictions, relating experiences to reading, establishing prior knowledge)

Credit: A.T.&T. Co. Photo Center

Talk about this photograph with a partner.

Write your answers on the lines.

1. Where are these people? _____

2. What are they doing? _____

3. Why are you in this class? _____

4. Why is education important for your job? _____

   _____

5. Do you plan to take more courses? _____

Reading About Work

Changes at the Workplace

Stefano hung up his jacket in his locker and started down the hallway to his position at the conveyor belt. He liked his job as an inspector at Foodco Distribution Company. Foodco is a warehouse where trucks deliver food from many food companies. Then, Foodco workers load the food onto other trucks, which take it to stores. Stefano is responsible for checking the orders of food before the loaders put the food on the trucks. Last month, he completed three years at Foodco. During those three years, he received two promotions. He is looking forward to another one soon.

As Stefano approached the conveyor belt, he ran into Greeley, his supervisor. "Hi, Greeley! What's new?" Greeley answered, "Actually, Stefano, there *is* something new that we need to talk about. In the near future, we're going to change over to a computer system that will inspect the food shipments as they move along the conveyor belt."

Stefano looked very anxious. "But, Greeley . . . my job. . . ." Greeley smiled at Stefano, "Yes, we're going to eliminate the job that you have now. But we'll need someone to operate the computer and enter the shipment information into it." Stefano breathed a sigh of relief, but then he looked worried again. "Greeley, I don't know anything about computers."

Greeley answered, "I wasn't finished telling you about our plans. Stefano, we consider you a valuable employee, and we want to retrain you. We need to eliminate your job, not you. We're going to set up some computer training classes. You'll attend the classes to learn about the computer. It will be very important in the future to understand how to use this new technology. What do you think, Stefano?"

Stefano said, "It sounds great! I know that computers are very important, and I'm pleased that you chose me for the training. When do classes start?"

Greeley answered, "I'll schedule you for the training classes that start next month. After you complete your training, you'll be ready for your next promotion!"

Understanding New Words and Idioms
(expanding vocabulary, understanding new words through context)

Read the following pairs of sentences with a partner. Decide together if the meaning of the sentences is the same or different. Circle *same* or *different*.

1. Stefano went to his position at the conveyor belt.   *same*   *different*
    Stefano went to his position at the line that moves products from one place to another.

2. He was looking forward to another promotion.   *same*   *different*
    He was happily anticipating another promotion.

3. Stefano approached the conveyor belt.   *same*   *different*
    Stefano went near the conveyor belt.

4. We're going to eliminate the job that you have now.   *same*   *different*
    We're going to promote you immediately.

5. Stefano breathed a sigh of relief.   *same*   *different*
    Stefano continued to feel anxious.

6. A computer system will inspect the food shipments.   *same*   *different*
    A computer system will inspect loads of food ready to go to the trucks.

Understanding the Reading
(identifying details, checking literal comprehension)

Read the following story about Stefano. There are *ten* mistakes in it. Work with a partner and correct the mistakes. Cross out the words that are wrong, and write the correction above the mistake.

Stefano works at Foodco Distribution Company. Foodco is a factory, and Stefano is a packer. Stefano's job is to check the orders after the food is loaded onto trucks. Last month, he completed two years at Foodco. During that time, he received three promotions. Greeley is Stefano's co-worker. Greeley told Stefano that Foodco is going to eliminate the job that he has now. A computer will inspect the shipments of food. Stefano knows a lot about computers. He will attend classes to train on the conveyor belt. He is not very happy about the training classes. Greeley scheduled Stefano's training to start next week.

Discussing

Activity 1: Fact or opinion? *(distinguishing between fact and opinion)*

Read the following sentences with a partner. Decide if each sentence is a *fact* (something that you can prove) or an *opinion* (something that you think or believe). Put a check (✔) under *fact* or *opinion*.

		Fact	Opinion
1.	Extra training is necessary for promotions in many jobs.	✔	
2.	If you want to get a promotion, your boss has to like you.		
3.	Training is always done at the workplace.		
4.	It is often necessary to take more training because there are many changes in the workplace.		
5.	You can check your community college catalog for information about courses and tuition.		
6.	The community college nearest your house is the best one.		
7.	You should take only courses that will help you make more money.		
8.	A counselor at the community college can help you choose courses.		
9.	Courses such as French, photography, or sewing will never help you in your life.		

Activity 2: Talking about training and education plans (*discussing goals, taking notes, reporting information to class, filling in a chart*)

In groups of three or four, discuss these questions about job training and education goals. One member of the group will be the secretary and write down the group's answers on the chart. Another member of the group will be the reporter and report the group's answers to the class.

1.   What kind of job training did you receive when you started your job?

2.   Were there changes on your job that made it necessary for you to receive more training? Will you receive more job training in the future?

3.   Did you ever take job-related courses at a community college? What kind of courses did you take? Do you plan to take any job-related courses in the future?

4.   Did you ever take personal-interest classes at a community college? What kind of classes did you take? Do you plan to take any personal-interest classes in the future?

Name	Job Training	Additional Job Training	Job-Related Courses	Personal Interest Courses

Reading at Work

Understanding New Words

(expanding vocabulary, understanding words through context)

Read the sentences below. Find and circle the underlined words in the reading.

1. Before a person can take Advanced Typing, he or she must take the prerequisite course—Beginning Typing.

2. A fitness class will help you to keep your body healthy and in good condition.

3. People who like to make things with their hands may decide to take a crafts class.

Understanding the Reading

(scanning to locate specific information)

On the following page are some courses from a community college continuing education catalog. These are *personal-interest* courses that people take because they are interested in the subjects. They do not receive college credit for these courses. Scan the course offerings and then write the answers to the questions.

1. Which class meets only one time? _____

2. Which class has a prerequisite? _____

3. Which class do you need to bring something to?_____

4. Which course(s) can help you when you travel?_____

   _____

5. Can a person take both Beginning Conversational Italian and Basic

   Photography in the same semester?_____

   Why or why not?_____

6. Can a person take both Beginning Yoga and Japanese Cooking in the same

   semester? _____

   Why or why not?_____

7. Can a person take both Beginning Cake Decorating and Japanese Cooking

   in the same semester? _____

   Why or why not?_____

8. Which class is the most expensive? _____

9. Which class is the cheapest? _____

10. How many courses have more than one section? _____

LANGUAGE

Intermediate Conversational German
Learn German vocabulary and improve your grammar skills so that you can understand and speak in more advanced conversations. We'll include excellent practice situations for the business person, the traveler, or the student interested in self-improvement. Prerequisite: GERC01, Beginning Conversational German or equivalent.

GER C03 35

Meets Thursdays, Sept. 20 - Nov. 29, 7-9:45 P.M. Room 380.   24.00

Beginning Conversational Italian
If you want to be able to carry on simple conversations in Italian, this is the time to learn phrases regarding shopping, cuisine, clothing, travel, numbers and other everyday topics. Your speaking practice will be supplemented by presentations on Italian life, customs, dialects and cities of Italy.

ITL C02 35

Meets Mondays, Sept. 17 - Dec. 3, 7-9:45 P.M. Room 385.   24.00

PHOTOGRAPHY

Photography for Everyone
If you own a camera and want to take better pictures, this workshop is for you! We will cover the features of your camera and how they can be used to improve your snapshots. Whether you own a simple point-and-shoot camera or a sophisticated automatic system, you will benefit by learning how to avoid common mistakes. Also included will be tips on camera loading, handling and maintenance. Please bring your camera and accessories to class.

PHG C21 01

Meets Thursday, Dec. 13, 7-9:45 P.M. Room   303.
4.00

Basic Photography
If you have never operated an adjustable camera or feel unsure of its use, you can learn to take good pictures through an understanding of camera operation, exposure, film, composition and flash. Bring your own adjustable camera and instruction book to the first class. Plan to purchase your own film for several assignments.

PHG C02 20

Meets Thursdays, Sept. 20 - Oct. 25, 7-9:20 P.M. Room 118.   15.00

GAMES

Beginning Bridge
If you have played little or no bridge, this course will teach you the mechanics, fundamentals and basic concepts of bidding and card play. Begin playing this fascinating and complex game as quickly as possible. Skills learned in this course will last a lifetime.

REC C01 35

Meets Tuesdays, Sept. 18 - Nov. 6, 7:15-9:35 P.M. Room 422.   16.00

FITNESS

Beginning Yoga
Yoga is a system of physical exercise and mental relaxation as well as an attitude toward life. You will gain peace of mind and the ability to relax as you improve muscle tone and body flexibility. Learn how to cope with stress and tension via this coed class. Bring mat or towel to class.

REC C18 35

Meets Wednesdays, Sept. 19 - Dec. 5, 6:30-7:50 P.M. Gym.   12.00

Dancercise
Trim inches while having fun. Dancercise is a fitness/dance program designed to strengthen the heart and lungs, trim and tone the entire body, increase flexibility, improve coordination and develop body awareness. Together we will work to exercise out the stresses and strains of daily living.

PED C46 35

Meets Tuesdays and Thursdays, Sept. 20 - Dec. 13, 8-8:50 P.M. Gym.   13.00

FOODS

Japanese Cooking
Bring a bit of the Orient to your table. Learn to create exotic Japanese cuisine with minimum effort. All courses of a Japanese meal will be included in the recipe demonstration.

HEC C39 35

Meets Wednesdays, Nov. 7 - Dec. 5, 7-9:45 P.M. Room 419.   27.00

Beginning Cake Decorating
Discover the beautiful art of cake decorating. It's easy and fun. You will learn how to prepare the cakes for decoration and prepare various frostings for each type of decoration. Learn sugar moldings, flowers, borders and basic decoration with attractive uses of color. Students will purchase equipment after the first class session.

HEC C09 35

Meets Tuesdays, Oct. 30 - Dec. 4, 7-10 P.M. Room 114.
22.00

Meets Wednesdays, Sept. 19 - Nov. 28, 7-9:45 P.M. Room 242.   24.00

CRAFTS

Woodcarving
Design and produce a project in woodcarving or wood sculpture. You'll receive individual instruction in selection of materials and use and maintenance of tools such as knives, gouges, and chisels. Tools and materials may be purchased through your instructor.

WOT C03 30

Meets Thursdays, Sept. 20 - Nov. 29, 7-9:45 P.M. Room 149. $71.00/71.00/24.00* *Touch Tone #5433*

WOT C03 35

Meets Wednesdays, Sept. 19 - Nov. 28, 7-9:45 P.M. Room 196.   24.00

Listening
(listening for specific information, filling in a chart)

Teresa, LaShanda, Johnnie, and Soon work at Foodco. They are discussing their plans during their break. They each decided to take a personal-interest course at their community college. Listen to the tape and fill in the following chart.

	Course Name	Day(s)	Time	Fees	Start Date
Teresa	Beginning Cake Decorating				
LaShanda					
Soon					
Johnnie					

Writing
(filling out a form)

Choose one of the courses from the Reading at Work section. Fill in the following continuing education registration form for yourself.

CONTINUING EDUCATION REGISTRATION FORM

Please print.   __Male __Female   Name of college previously attended

Social Security number _____   _____

Name _____   Name of high school/Year of graduation
    last   first   middle
Address _____   _____

City _____ State _____ Zip _____   GED certification_____

Telephone _____
       day   evening

Birth date _____

Signature _____

COURSE NO.	SECT.	COURSE TITLE	LOCATION	DAY	TIME	ROOM	TUITION
/							
/							
/							
/							

Registration fee $5.00
Total

Status: (check one)
- □ 1. Never before enrolled
- □ 2. Enrolled last semester
- □ 3. Previously enrolled

Present college:
- □ 4. Public two-year
- □ 5. Public four-year
- □ 6. Private two-year
- □ 7. Private four-year

Student intent: (check one)
- □ 1. To prepare for a new or first career
- □ 2. To improve present skills
- □ 3. To explore courses to decide on a career
- □ 4. To prepare for transfer to a four-year college
- □ 5. To remedy basic skill deficiencies
- □ 6. To pursue non-career, personal interests
- □ 7. To prepare for high school diploma equivalence
- □ 8. Other

Ethnic code: (check one)
- □ 1. Asian/Pacific Islander
- □ 2. American Indian/ Alaskan Native
- □ 3. Black/Non-Hispanic
- □ 4. Hispanic
- □ 5. White/Non-Hispanic
- □ 6. Non-resident/Alien
- □ 7. No response

Current employment status: (check one)
- □ 1. Employed full time
- □ 2. Employed part time, over 15 hours/week
- □ 3. Employed part time, less than 15 hours/week
- □ 4. Homemaker
- □ 5. Unemployed
- □ 6. Other/No response

For VISA or MasterCard payment only: Bring registration and payment to:

Using Math

(reading charts and order forms, adding and subtracting whole numbers, plotting information on a chart)

Foodco needs to maintain certain amounts of food (inventory) in the warehouse. It doesn't want to keep too much inventory, and it doesn't want to be short of food either. The warehouse manager calculated an acceptable *range* of inventory for each kind of food. If the inventory of a food falls below the low point, Stefano needs to order more immediately. If there is a large amount of inventory, then Stefano doesn't need to reorder immediately; but Foodco needs to reevaluate its range for that food. Following is the range for each food in the warehouse. The shaded area shows the "safest" amounts.

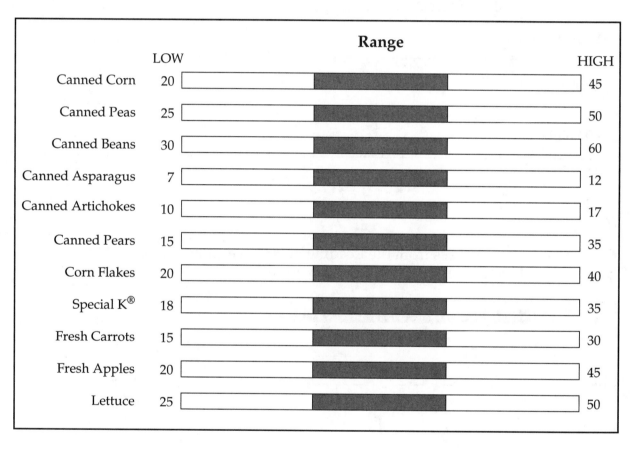

Range

	LOW		HIGH
Canned Corn	20		45
Canned Peas	25		50
Canned Beans	30		60
Canned Asparagus	7		12
Canned Artichokes	10		17
Canned Pears	15		35
Corn Flakes	20		40
Special K®	18		35
Fresh Carrots	15		30
Fresh Apples	20		45
Lettuce	25		50

Do the following activities with a partner.

A. Read the following order forms and fill in the chart on page 118 with each store's orders.

B. Figure out how much inventory remains at the end of the day. Fill in the numbers on the chart on page 118. (*Hint:* Add all of the orders for each food. Then subtract the total orders from the beginning inventory of each food to find the ending inventory.)

C. Plot the number of ending inventory (use an *x*) for each food on the range line (on page 114). Where does the ending inventory for each food fall? In the "safe" area? In the "low" area? In the "high" area?

D. Which foods does Stefano need to reorder for tomorrow's shipments?

_____

_____

Foodco Distribution Center

123 Anystreet
Anycity, Anystate 12345

Shipping Form

Date: August 11, 1993   **Ship on:** August 12, 1993

Ship To: Diamond Foods   **Phone:** 555–1234

QUANTITY # of Cases	TYPE OF FOOD	LOADED	UNIT PRICE	TOTAL PRICE
10	Canned Corn	✔	~	~
7	Canned Peas	✔	~	~
1	Canned Artichokes	✔	~	~
13	Fresh Carrots	✔	~	~
9	Fresh Apples	✔	~	~

Foodco Distribution Center
123 Anystreet
Anycity, Anystate 12345

Shipping Form

Date: August 11, 1993   **Ship on:** August 12, 1993

Ship To: P+A   **Phone:** 555-9033

QUANTITY # of Cases	TYPE OF FOOD	LOADED	UNIT PRICE	TOTAL PRICE
5	Canned Peas	✔	~	~
3	Canned Beans	✔	~	~
1	Canned Asparagus	✔	~	~
4	Corn Flakes	✔	~	~
5	Fresh Carrots	✔	~	~
7	Lettuce	✔	~	~

Foodco Distribution Center
123 Anystreet
Anycity, Anystate 12345

Shipping Form

Date: August 11, 1993   **Ship on:** August 12, 1993

Ship To: Six-Ten   **Phone:** 555-7500

QUANTITY # of Cases	TYPE OF FOOD	LOADED	UNIT PRICE	TOTAL PRICE
2	Canned Corn	✔	~	~
1	Canned Beans	✔	~	~
1	Special K®	✔	~	~
1	Fresh Carrots	✔	~	~
1	Fresh Apples	✔	~	~

Foodco Distribution Center
123 Anystreet
Anycity, Anystate 12345

Shipping Form

Date: August 11, 1993   **Ship on:** August 12, 1993

Ship To: Bargain Buy   **Phone:** 555–4811

QUANTITY # of Cases	TYPE OF FOOD	LOADED	UNIT PRICE	TOTAL PRICE
30	Canned Corn	✔	~	~
30	Canned Peas	✔	~	~
30	Canned Beans	✔	~	~
8	Canned Pears	✔	~	~
8	Corn Flakes	✔	~	~
6	Special K®	✔	~	~
12	Fresh Carrots	✔	~	~
15	Fresh Apples	✔	~	~
10	Lettuce	✔	~	~

Foodco Distribution Center
123 Anystreet
Anycity, Anystate 12345

Shipping Form

Date: August 11, 1993   **Ship on:** August 12, 1993

Ship To: Super Big   **Phone:** 555–2000

QUANTITY # of Cases	TYPE OF FOOD	LOADED	UNIT PRICE	TOTAL PRICE
50	Canned Corn	✔	~	~
43	Canned Peas	✔	~	~
27	Canned Beans	✔	~	~
3	Canned Asparagus	✔	~	~
2	Canned Artichokes	✔	~	~
37	Canned Pears	✔	~	~
21	Corn Flakes	✔	~	~
15	Special K®	✔	~	~
20	Fresh Carrots	✔	~	~
17	Fresh Apples	✔	~	~
16	Lettuce	✔	~	~

AUG 12 5:00 A.M.

Beginning Inventory (# of Cases)		STORES					Ending Inventory (# of Cases)
		Diamond	P&A	Six-Ten	Bargain Buy	Super Big	
Canned Corn	125	10					
Canned Peas	130	7					
Canned Beans	95						
Canned Asparagus	10						
Canned Artichokes	12						
Canned Pears	80						
Corn Flakes	64						
Special K®	57						
Fresh Carrots	75						
Fresh Apples	83						
Lettuce	60						

Audio Tape Scripts

Unit 1—Listening
Student Text Pages 8–9

MRS. SMITH: You've got a small shift today, Tom. The flu is going around the bakery, and four of your people called in sick. So we have to change the crews. Let's see, you have four people on each crew, right?

TOM: Yeah. But we rotate the people on each crew, so almost everyone has some experience on each job. Which people are sick?

MRS. SMITH: Uhm, let me check. Let's see . . . José Gomez, Liu Chen, Teresa Witkowski and Marie Andropoulos all have the flu.

TOM: Well, this is a bit of a problem. José and Liu are both dough mixers and Teresa and Marie are both inspectors at the end of the line.

MRS. SMITH: You'll need to combine the crews and operate only two machines today instead of three. Let's see if we can make some changes.

TOM: Well, Tyree Washington is usually a machine operator, but he also has experience as an inspector. And Rosa Garcia has worked as a machine operator. But, wait, I already have two machine operators, so Rosa can continue in her packing job. Diane is a packer now, but she started as a dough mixer. I think we've solved the problem. We can make two crews now. I'll go tell my workers.

Unit 2—Listening
Student Text Page 21

TAPE TRANSCRIPT:

(Voice of Miss McCormick)

All of the employees in the Jewelry, Men's Furnishings, Housewares, and Domestics Departments take their breaks between 10:00 and 11:00 in the morning. Each break is 15 minutes long. Jewelry and Men's Furnishings take their breaks between 10:00 and 10:30. The other two departments— Housewares and Domestics—take their breaks between 10:30 and 11:00. When you make the schedule of the breaks, it is important that both employees from one department do *not* take their breaks at the same time. Now, let's see . . . Jewelry and Men's Furnishings take their break from 10:00 to 10:30. Letty likes to go first, so put her from 10:00 to 10:15. George likes to wait, so he'll take his break from 10:15 to 10:30. I think you can finish the schedule for Jewelry and Men's Furnishings now. Housewares and Domestics take their break between 10:30 and 11:00. Fred and Brenda always go on break together, so let them take their break from 10:30 to 10:45. I think that you have enough information to finish the morning schedule.

Please make a schedule for afternoon breaks, too, following the same timetable. The afternoon breaks are between 2:00 and 3:00.

Unit 3—Listening
Student Text Page 36

MR. GRAY: Welcome to the ABC Steel Company, Anthony and Henry. We're glad that you've decided to work for us. As the safety manager, I want you to know that we are very concerned about our employees' safety, and we try very hard to provide a safe environment for our employees. On our video for new employees that you saw this morning, two of the most important points that we want our employees to learn is to report all problems and to ask questions when you don't understand instructions.

Now, let's see . . . let's talk about safety equipment. First of all, I'm glad to see that both of you are wearing proper work clothes—not too tight and not too loose. I'm going to issue each of you a hard hat which you will need to wear all the time in the steel mill. Both of you will also need safety glasses which are always necessary in the mill. Shoes with safety toe caps are necessary for all employees in case a heavy object falls on your foot.

In addition, Henry, you will need safety goggles and a respirator to use when you are painting. You'll need a special paint jacket to wear, too. I'm also going to issue you leather gloves to protect your hands from the sharp edges of the steel.

Anthony, since you're our new electrician, you'll need rubber boots and rubber gloves for protection when working with electricity. Here's an equipment belt to hold your tools and a safety belt, too, in case you need to tie yourself to a wire. Then you'll have your hands free to work.

Oh, I almost forgot—each ABC Steel employee receives a pair of earplugs because of the loud noise at the worksite.

I'm glad to see that neither of you is wearing jewelry. ABC Steel has a company policy that says employees cannot wear jewelry in the workplace.

I see Mr. Jackson coming. He's your supervisor, Henry, and, Anthony, there's your supervisor, Mr. Taylor. They'll take you to your work stations. Good luck, and remember, safety first!

Unit 4—Listening
Student Text Page 50

ROSA: Let's make sure that we have everything ready for the party, Mattie. Kathy will be leaving at the end of next week. We still need to order the food and buy the gift. Let's see—we decided to have the party during lunch next Friday, right?

MATTIE: Right, Rosa! Now, where's the sign-up list? Are we going to have the main dishes catered?

ROSA: I've got the list here. Yes, I called the caterer, and he's going to bring roast beef, chicken, and potato salad.

MATTIE: Okay, and I see that almost everyone signed up to bring something. Oh, no one is bringing fruit. And nobody signed up to bring utensils.

ROSA: Well, I haven't talked to everyone yet. But Mario is going to bring his famous pizza. And Nadia promised to make her special tacos. Lisa has a recipe for a new salad that she wants to try.

MATTIE: Is Chen going to make his delicious egg rolls?

ROSA: Yes, he is. But most of the men have decided not to cook. Jack is bringing paper plates, John is bringing napkins, Kristofer is bringing soft drinks, and Fernando is bringing potato chips. Debbie wants to bring fresh vegetables like carrots and celery. I'm going to bring a dessert—German chocolate cake.

MATTIE: Great! You make the best German chocolate cake, Rosa! I'll bring a dessert too—chocolate chip cookies are my specialty. And Nola told me that she is going to make a cheesecake. Okay. The food is taken care of. Now, how about the gift? How much should we spend?

ROSA: Well, the caterer is going to cost $42.00. There are 14 of us, and if we each contribute $5.00, we can buy a present for $25.00 and still have money for the wrapping paper and card.

MATTIE: When I see Tomás at break, I'll ask him if he can bring the utensils, and Eva can bring the fruit.

ROSA: Good! Then everything will be ready for the party! Time to get back to work!

Unit 5—Listening
Student Text Page 58

MR. COATES: Hi, there, Joe! How's it going?

JOE: Fine, Mr. Coates. Fred said that you have a special job for me. What do you want me to do?

MR. COATES: Well, you've been unloading heavy boxes all afternoon. Take a break from that hard work. Why don't you help me check in these boxes? Our warehouse has been making a lot of mistakes lately, and I need to check the inventory numbers of these boxes before you take them to the departments in the store.

JOE: Sure, Mr. Coates. I'd like a break from lifting the boxes. One thing, though—could you say the numbers and letters slowly? Sometimes I get confused with the letters and numbers in English.

MR. COATES: (laughing) I'll try, Joe. If I start to go too fast, slow me down. Okay. Here's the inventory list. Check off the numbers that I read to you. Now, there are 20 inventory numbers on the list, but I see only 10 boxes. Let's see which ones we have. Ready?

JOE: Ready.

MR. COATES: The first number is A 60 F 09. Got that? Okay. Next is B 40 C 82. Then E 60 F 09. Everything Okay?

JOE: Okay so far.

MR. COATES: Next is K 27 I 55. Then M 03 H 78. Z 90 T 41.
(Starts to go faster.) Y 35 C 19. I 80 H 37—

JOE: I'm lost, Mr. Coates! Could you repeat that last number? I think that you're going a little too fast.

MR. COATES: Sorry, Joe. I got carried away. The last number was I 80 H 37. Then V 30 S 57. Let's see, there's one box left and that is Q 50 A 73. Do you have 10 boxes checked off?

JOE: Yes. Now, what order do you want them in?

MR. COATES: I want you to make two stacks with 5 boxes in each stack. So number the boxes 1–10, and put boxes 1–5 in one stack and boxes 6–10 in the second stack. Then you can put the two stacks on the cart and take them into the store.

JOE: Okay. What's the first box?

MR. COATES: Here's the order that I want them in—

The first box is Z 90 T 41

The second box is E 60 F 09

The third box is K 27 I 55

The fourth box is Q 50 A 73

And the fifth box is A 60 F 09

The sixth box is Y 35 C 19

Number seven is B 40 C 82

Let's see—number eight is I 80 H 37

And the ninth box is M 03 H 78

And the last box—number 10—is V 30 S 57

Do you want me to read them again?

JOE: Well, I feel pretty confident that I've got them in the right order, but it's probably a good idea to read them again.

MR. COATES: It's always a good idea to check your work. You've got a good head on your shoulders, Joe! Let me give those numbers to you again.

The first box is Z 90 T 41.

The second box is E 60 F 09.

The third box is K 27 I 55.

The fourth box is Q 50 A 73.

The fifth box is A 60 F 09.

The sixth box is Y 35 C 19.

The seventh box is B 40 C 82.

The eighth box is I 80 H 37.

The ninth box is M 03 H 78.

The tenth box is V 30 S 57.

Unit 6—Listening
Student Text Page 71

MRS. SIMS:	I'm so glad that you've joined our team, Mark. You'll enjoy working with my other employees, Tom and Sammy. Delivering those trays and cleaning the kitchen can be hard work, but Tom and Sammy are wonderful co-workers! Now, I'll introduce you to the other members of the food service team. Ms. Black over here is in charge of food preparation. She has four employees working for her.
MS. BLACK:	How do you do, Mark!
MARK:	Nice to meet you, Ms. Black.
MRS. SIMS:	And here are the cooks. Linda, meet Mark.
LINDA:	Hi, Mark!
MARK:	Glad to meet you, Linda!
MRS. SIMS:	This is Beverly, Mark.
MARK:	Nice to meet you, Beverly.
BEVERLY:	Be seeing you around, Mark.
MRS. SIMS:	Michiko, say "hi" to Mark.
MICHIKO:	Hello, glad to meet you.
MARK:	Hi, Michiko!
MRS. SIMS:	Robert, this is Mark, my new employee.
ROBERT:	How's it going, Mark?
MARK:	Great! Catch you later, Robert!
MRS. SIMS:	In this office is Mr. Anderson. He's in charge of ordering all of the food. Mr. Anderson, I'd like you to meet Mark, the new member of my team.
MR. ANDERSON:	Hi, Mark! Welcome aboard!
MARK:	How do you do?
MRS. SIMS:	Where are Juan and Tony, Bill?
MR. ANDERSON:	They're out checking orders at Shipping and Receiving. We just got a big shipment from one of our suppliers.
MRS. SIMS:	Well, Mark, I guess that you'll have to meet Mr. Anderson's two assistants later. See you at the meeting this afternoon, Bill! And, finally, in this little office is our accountant, Mr. Anderson. Would you believe that we have *two* Mr. Andersons? You met Bill Anderson from the ordering department before, and this is Ned Anderson, the accountant. He pays the bills.
MR. ANDERSON:	How do you do, Mark?
MARK:	Nice to meet you, Mr. Anderson.
MR. ANDERSON:	And this is my assistant, Loretta.
LORETTA:	Hi, Mark!
MARK:	Hi, Loretta!
MRS. SIMS:	(laughing) Did I say "finally" before? Well, I was wrong. We're not finished yet. I forgot Mr. Ortiz—he's in charge of *all* of food service. He's my boss, too! I'll take you to his office now.

Unit 7—Listening
Student Text Page 80

Mr. Gupta is the speaker throughout.

PART 1. I need to figure out how much money we made each day this week. But I don't seem to have all of the deposit slips here. Hm—let's see which ones I have in this bag. Oh, here's the Monday lunch deposit slip—$404.26. And here's Wednesday's breakfast—$321.75. And Thursday's dinner—$610.47. Not bad. Tuesday's breakfast was $293.51, and here's Friday's lunch—$538.24. That's always a big day for us. Now I wonder if the other deposit receipts are in that bag over there. Let's have a look. (Voice fades out.)

PART 2. I found five deposit slips in that first bag. I wonder how many are in this bag. Well, I see a few deposit slips here. Which ones are they? Here's Friday's dinner. We made $741.93. That was a good night! Oh, and here's Wednesday's lunch—$429.05. Another good meal. Hm—Monday's breakfast was $207.53. Monday morning is never very good for us. We'll need to work on that. And Tuesday's dinner was $584.61. That's not bad for the middle of the week. Thursday's breakfast was a lot better than Monday's. We made $313.78. Those are all the deposit slips here. Now there's one more place where the other slips might be. I'll check the file box. (Voice fades out.)

PART 3. Well, I've found 10 deposit slips so far. I hope that the last five are in this file box. I don't know where else to look. Ah ha! Here are the last deposit slips. Now I'll be able to figure out how much money we made during the week. Let's see— Wednesday's dinner. That was pretty good—$673.10. Hm, Friday's breakfast. Fridays are always one of our best days. We made $362.17 this week. And here's Thursday's lunch. Not bad—$457.03. Here's Monday's dinner. Monday is such a slow day. We made only $523.44 for dinner on Monday. And finally, Tuesday's lunch—$434.91. Great! Now I've got all the information. I can figure out how much we made each day and how much we made for the week.

Unit 8—Listening
Student Text Page 90–91

1. Kenji is making fries at Hamburger Heaven. He heats the oil to 335°. He fills the basket one-third full with potatoes. He puts the fry basket into the hot oil. He turns on the fry computer. He takes the fry basket out of the oil when the buzzer sounds. He drains the fries for five seconds. He throws away the cooked fries after six minutes.

2. Ali is taking orders at the counter at Hamburger Heaven. He smiles and greets his customer. He listens to the order, repeats it into the microphone, and enters it into the cash register. He doesn't understand exactly how many and what size drinks the customer wants, so he repeats the drink order back to the customer. He rings the total on the cash register—$5.28. He tells the customer the total. The customer gives Ali a twenty-dollar bill, and Ali immediately puts the money in the register. He then counts $14.72 in change for the customer. He hands the tray to the customer and thanks the customer.

3. Yvette works at the Favorite Toys Company. She assembles dolls. Today she is assembling the Allison Doll. She is fitting the arms, legs, and head to the body. She fits Part A into Part B. Then she fits Part C into Part D. Next, she fits Part E into Part F, and Part G into Part H. Finally, she fits Part I into Part J. To meet her goal, Yvette needs to assemble one doll every minute. This morning, she assembled 112 dolls in two hours, which includes 10 minutes for break.

4. Ula works in housekeeping at Eastlake Hospital. Her job is to make the patients' beds. She loads her cart with linens in the supply room. The sheets and pillowcases are folded in bundles of ten. Ula takes 20 bundles of sheets and 10 bundles of pillowcases. The blankets are folded in bundles of five. Ula takes 19 bundles of blankets. This afternoon she makes 95 beds in 4½ hours.

Unit 9—Listening
Student Text Page 101

Ida gets up at 6:00 every weekday. She washes a load of clothes before she makes breakfast at 7:00 for her family. She takes her 4-year-old daughter to the daycare center at 8:00, and she takes her 6-year-old son to school at 8:15. She starts work at 8:30 every weekday, and she finishes at 5:00. At 5:30, she picks up her daughter at the daycare center. At 5:45, she picks up her son at her neighbor's house. Every evening, she makes supper at about 6:00.

Monday was a busy day for Ida. She had to leave work at noon during her lunch hour to buy a birthday present and a card for a co-worker. In the evening, she went to the library to study for a test that she was going to have in her computer class. She was at the library from 7:30–9:30.

On Tuesday evening, she went to her computer class from 7:00–8:30.

On Wednesday, she left work during her lunch hour to go to the post office and cleaners. After supper that evening, Ida went to the computer lab to work on a project for her class. She was there from 7:00–10:00.

On Thursday, she left work early at 4:00 to go to a parent/teacher conference at her son's school. That evening, she went to her computer class again from 7:00–8:30. After her computer class, she went to Diamond Foods to buy groceries. She got home at 10:00.

At 9:00 on Friday morning, she met with her supervisor to discuss the possibilities of a promotion. Ida was very tired after work on Friday. She took her family to Hamburger Heaven for supper at 6:30.

Unit 10—Listening
Student Text Page 113

TERESA: There are so many courses that I want to take! I didn't know that it was possible to study so many different things! I had a hard time deciding between Beginning Cake Decorating and Japanese Cooking.

LASHANDA: So, what did you decide to take, Teresa?

TERESA: Well, I decided that first I wanted to learn how to decorate cakes.

LASHANDA: Oh, good! Maybe we'll be in the same class! When is your class?

TERESA: It's on Tuesdays from 7–9:45. What about yours, Lashanda?

LASHANDA: Darn! I can't go on Tuesdays. I have a babysitting problem on Tuesdays. I'm taking my cake decorating class on Wednesdays from 7–9:45.

SOON: You'll like the cake decorating class. I already took it. Now I'm going to take a photography course on Thursdays from 7–9:20. That fits into my schedule really well! Someday, when I'm a famous photographer, you can say that you knew Soon Park when you worked at Foodco!

JOHNNIE: Well, if you ladies need any carpentry work in the future, just call on me. I'm going to take a woodcarving class. Say, LaShanda, maybe we can carpool. My class is on Wednesdays from 7–9:45, too. When does your class start?

LASHANDA: Let's see. . . . it starts on Wednesday, September 19. How about yours?

JOHNNIE: Yes—same day!

TERESA: Look at this—my course starts on October 30. Why does it start so late?

SOON: Well, some classes are only six weeks long. For example, my class starts on Thursday, September 20, and it finishes on Thursday, October 25. Then, if I want, I can register for another class. I might take Intermediate Photography. You know, one of the great things about taking classes at our community college is that they are so cheap. You can learn about so many different things at bargain prices. My photography class is only $15.00.

JOHNNIE: That's true. My class is a little more expensive because I have to buy supplies, too. But still, it's only $24.00.

LASHANDA: Teresa and I need to pay $22.00. But, that's a lot cheaper than private lessons. This way I can find out if I like something before I spend a lot of money!

TERESA: Let's try to arrange things so that we can all be in a class together next semester! Say, how about an exercise class? It'll be right after the holidays and you know how it is after eating all those holiday sweets. . . . (voice fades)

Skills Index

The skills listed below are introduced and/or emphasized on the pages indicated.

Functional Literacy Skills

Information
Completing Safety Signs, 33
Figuring Out a Schedule, 102
Identifying Signs, 27
Labeling a Picture, 18–19
Proofreading, 88
Reading an Information Chart, 64
Reading and Understanding an Earnings Statement, 59
Scanning to Locate Specific Information, 48, 88, 111–112

Reading at Work
Reading an Article in a Company Newsletter, 57, 79, 89, 100
Reading a Safety Survey, 34–35
Reading and Understanding a Company Policy Manual, 7–8
Reading Instructions for Operating a Photocopy Machine, 20
Reading from a Training Manual, 70
Scanning a Company Newsletter, 48
Scanning a Page from a Continuing Education Catalog, 111–112

Listening Skills
Differentiating Numbers, Letters, and Names, 8–9, 21, 50, 58, 71, 80, 90–91, 101, 113
Listening for Specific Information, 8–9, 21, 36, 45–46, 50, 58, 71, 80, 101, 113
Listening for Specific Information to Solve Problems, 8–9, 21, 50, 80, 91
Listening to Verify Information, 58, 90–91
Understanding Context Clues, 45–46

Math and Graphical Literacy Skills

Charts and Tables
Completing a Chart, 78
Filling in a Chart, 80
Filling in a Table, 72–73
Plotting Information on a Chart, 114
Reading about and Interpreting a Flow Chart, 23–24
Reading and Interpreting a Table, 72
Reading Charts and Order Forms, 114–118

Decimals
Adding, Subtracting, and Multiplying Decimals, 60–62
Multiplying Decimals, 72–73

Diagrams
Discussing and Interpreting a Diagram of a Cash Register, 22

Speaking Skills

Writing Skills

Text Credits

Unit 1, page 7—Adapted from Agreement Between Chicago Heights Steel, Inc. and United Steelworkers of America. Used with permission.

Unit 2, pages 18, 19, 20—Adapted from Canon NP-3225/3225F Operator's Manual. Used with permission.

Unit 3, page 32—Safety Statistics from *You and Safety* ©1983 and *About Materials Handling Safety* ©1980 by Channing L. Bete Co., Inc., South Deerfield, MA 01373. Used with permission.

Unit 3, page 34—Adapted from U.S. Department of Labor—Federal Employees' Notice of Traumatic Injury and Claim for Continuation of Pay/Compensation.

Unit 3, page 35—Adapted from "What's Your Safety Score?" ©1988 Parplay International. Used with permission.

Unit 4, page 49—Adapted from "The Chicago Rev-iew" (The IRS Newsletter), August 1990. Names and places changed.

Unit 5, page 57—Adapted from "The Open Door of Communication," Kohl's Update, July 1990. Used with permission.

Unit 6, page 70—Adapted from Radisson Hotels International *Yes, I Can* (Unit 5): Understanding Yourself. Used with permission.

Unit 7, page 79—Adapted from "Inventory Shortage Reduction," Kohl's Update, July 1990. Used with permission.

Unit 8, page 89—From Kohl's Konnection, April 1989. Used with permission.

Unit 10, page 112—Adapted from Triton College (River Grove, IL) Continuing Education Class Schedule, Fall 1990. Used with permission.

Unit 10, page 113—Modified Triton College (River Grove, IL) Continuing Education Registration Form, Fall 1990. Used with permission.